Park St.

£2-99

C000133146

THE CTC BOOK OF CYCLE TOURING

The CTC Book of
CYCLE TOURING

LES WOODLAND

in Association with the
Cyclists' Touring Club

The Crowood Press

First published in 1995 by
The Crowood Press Ltd
Ramsbury, Marlborough
Wiltshire SN8 2HR

© Les Woodland 1995

All rights reserved. No part of this publication may
be reproduced or transmitted in any form or by any means,
electronic or mechanical, including photocopy, recording,
or any information storage and retrieval system, without
permission in writing from the publishers.

The right of Les Woodland to be identified as the author of this work has
been asserted by him in accordance with the Copyright, Designs and
Patents Act 1988.

British Library Cataloguing in Publication Data
A catalogue record for this book is available from the British Library.

ISBN 1 85223 925 5

Picture Credits
All photographs by the author unless otherwise stated

Typeset by Phoenix Typesetting, Ilkley, West Yorkshire.
Printed and bound by The Bath Press

Contents

Foreword

By the late 1880s our country roads were dominated by the bicycle. Its development by ingenious Victorian engineers presented the populace with the legendary winged heels of Mercury. The ability to propel oneself over previously undreamed-of distances in a comparatively short space of time significantly changed society. People were released from the grimy towns and cities to escape into a land of meadows, woods and rolling hills many had never seen before. Freedom to roam brought with it freedom of the spirit.

Today that freedom to wander the land by bicycle, discovering far-off places and people, attracts ever-growing numbers seeking relief from the pressures of modern life. As with any long-established activity, cycle touring has amassed a wealth of experiences as to how, and how not, to go about things. Since 1878 the Cyclists' Touring Club, Britain's oldest and largest cycling organization, has passed on this collected widsom to each successive new generation of cycle wanderers. In this book Les Woodland, in collaboration with the CTC, reveals the mysteries at the heart of the 'lore of the road'. A self-confessed unregenerated cycling itinerant with a penchant for sleeping in telephone boxes, Les has had more miles pass under his wheels than most. Presented with his first bicycle at a tender age by parents who confidently predicted its resale in a matter of weeks, he promptly embarked on a cycling career of ferocious dedication. Of all the lessons he learned, many the hard way, the most significant was that cycling was quite simply a lot of fun. Thus this book is no mere sanctimonious list of do's and don'ts but an entertaining celebration of the enjoyment to be gained from venturing out awheel. As the text develops Les expounds on his favourite 28 'golden rules' for successful cycle touring. In between you will learn all that a lifetime of vagrancy can bestow.

Cycling attracts people of all ages and from all walks of life, from the quiet 5 mile lane potterer to the 100 plus miles a day road-eater. In 1887 Thomas Stevens became the first to cycle right around the world. Even if your own ambition goes no further than covering the distance to the nearest country pub, this book will help you get the maximum enjoyment from your rides. Should you set your sights on longer journeys, involving the seeking out of overnight accommodation, Les Woodland's long experience of identifying the most convivial establishments will stand you in good stead.

Cycle touring is, perhaps, one of the last great freedoms. The road begins at your front doorstep or garden gate and leads wherever you will. Approached in the Woodland way, life on that road can be as carefree as you may wish. For sure there can be the occasional mishap, the odd mechanical difficulty and, as we all know, the sun doesn't always shine. Within these pages Les shows how to make light of such problems as can sometimes arise. Cycle touring teaches self-reliance and resourcefulness. It brings all the glorious variety of the countryside, and all within it, into a fresh perspective. It encourages health and fitness. As Les Woodland's experience has shown, it is also extremely habit-forming. Those not wishing to risk addiction should read no further. To those who seek adventure and the richest of experiences – let's ride!

Alan Harlow
Director, Cyclists' Touring Club
1995

1

Exit an Adonis

I couldn't have been paying attention. Suddenly all the cycling mags have filled with wheel-gods in Lycra – and I'm having trouble maintaining my self-assumed status in the village as Adonis-on-Wheels. I have just to pedal down the lane as if only warm cloud kept my wheels from the road and there'll be a swish and a light scent of embrocation and An Athlete will pedal by covered in foreign words.

It's not that I mind (apart from my self-esteem). After all, one reason for *being* a cyclist over the centuries has been to dress in gaudy clothes and act conspicuously. And to irritate people. The Pickwick Bicycle Club encouraged blades on penny-farthings to ride uniformed and bugling into distant villages. They'd lounge on the green before sending telegrams home merely to prove they'd got there. The aggravation they caused explains why small boys pushed sticks into their wheels, to watch the nobs sail over the handlebars. And cyclists' historical flirting with the *avant-garde* is why women began wearing bloomers or, worse . . . tights! The hussies.

These flashy kingfishers have history on their side. They deserve their place in the magazines along with the talk of chain-suck and hydraulic rock-shock-stoppin' suspensions. But don't you think they've missed the point? All you need to be a cyclist is a bike and half an hour to spare. People have crossed the Alps on single-geared roadsters with a basket on the front, like district nurses on holiday. They sweated, but they had a good time. They'd have enjoyed it more with 18 gears, pulling their levers like the signalman at Euston station, but – and this is the point – they did it, without all that. When bike-buyers in flat-as-old-beer Wisbech buy machines with names like Montana Sunshine Ultra Peak-Buster, they miss that truth (or were they misled by the mags?) And not just them. The *Eastern Daily Press* sought to publicize a ride by the Norwich branch of the Cyclists' Touring Club by publishing a photo of aggressive young men riding in Lycra and bulbous helmets along Great Yarmouth promenade. I don't know whom it encouraged but I suspect they were disappointed. CTC rides are conducive to coffee stops and the sniffing of cuckoopints.

A bargain at £2. I rescued this 1960s Moulton from a country auction, where the auctioneer whacked it with a stick and pronounced it 'some sort of ladies' bike, I think, or maybe a children's bike'. Bidding started at £1 and the opposition dropped out when I offered £2. It needs some work, of course, but it's an example of one of the trendiest bikes of its day and the first with effective suspension.

Nothing separates you from being what Americans call a 'leezure' cyclist but getting on your bike. And oddly, that's sometimes the hardest bit. Bernard Levin's consumption of digestive biscuits soared when he became a freelance writer. It wasn't that he *liked* digestive biscuits, just that there was always a better reason for eating them than getting on with his work. So you're not alone. That's why Nike devised the slogan 'Just do it'.

So go on, then – just do it. Get your bike out, pump the tyres, make sure the brakes work as well as those on the refrigerator lorry in front of you, and set off. Not that it's a good idea to cross the Alps at your first attempt. If Christopher Columbus had trial spins round the harbour before setting off for America, it doesn't seem unreasonable to keep your beginnings modest.

Not everybody realizes that. At thirteen I set off to ride 15 miles to

The old and the new – a traditional tandem, never out of fashion, and a mountain bike.

Rickmansworth, about which I knew little except that it sounded good and that a single main road connected it to my home. I packed three currant buns and pinned on a postcard reading 'Rickmansworth or Bust'. It was a heroic gesture. I'd eaten the first bun by Stanmore, convinced I'd ridden more than the mile and a half my clearly faulty cyclometer told me; I abandoned the attempt in Hatch End, listening to a café jukebox and struggling to eat the remaining buns without the owner seeing me. I can never hear Ned Miller sing 'From a Jack to a King' without recalling the awfulness of the ride home. Rickmansworth is fortunately a long word, so the writing on the postcard was small and caused minimum embarrassment.

The same can happen no matter how many years you've been cycling. The cartoonist Johnny Helms, whose optimistic-despite-it-all heroes have entertained readers of *Cycling Weekly* for forty years, showed his man Honk round-shouldered and exhausted at an estate agent's board which read: 'If You Lived Here, You'd Be Home By Now'. Decades later, stuck in traffic on the Chelmsford by-pass, I saw the same message on an advertisement for a housing estate.

So don't ride too far too soon. But then again don't give up just because *any* distance sounds a long way. People never believe how far you've been anyway. I've come home from a day in the wind and rain, red-eyed and strewn with grit and clearly shattered, only to meet visiting aunts who'd arrived in a Cortina with velour cushions and Radio 2 on the wireless.

'And how far did you go, Leslie?' they'd ask, using the name employed only by relatives who remember me in short trousers.

'Eighty miles, maybe,' I'd say, shrugging feebly and trying to sound modest about it. Any cyclist would have believed it immediately from the shell-shocked eyes and the slumping spine and the rain-soaked shoes.

'Eight miles?' they'd say. 'Well, well . . .'. But the 'well, well' was in that special tone which also meant 'Leslie, don't you think you're a little too grown-up now for telling fibs like that?'

But you *can* ride eighty miles on a bicycle. You can ride a hundred miles, and not always with unbecoming distress. I once rode 198 miles and spent the night asleep in my Austin Allegro, not realizing that a spin round the car park would have got me to 200 miles for the only time in my life.

Alan Leng, the former director of the CTC, once told me: 'Most people would be astonished how far they could ride if they wanted. After all, it's difficult to ride at less than 8 miles an hour – you'd fall off. So if you're out from 9 until 6, you can ride forty miles in 5 hours and have almost as long again for lunch, cups of tea or dangling your feet in a stream.'

Fitness

The more you ride, the fitter you get. And the slower you ride (within reason), the further you go, provided you've got the time to complete the journey. Never hurry unless you have to.

> **Rule 1** *Ride slower than you'd imagine, more often than you'd expect, and never as far as you'd like.*

The time will come when you'll knock off long distances without thinking about it. I spent an evening once with two of the sport's great magazine editors, Alan Gayfer of *Cycling* and Jock Wadley of *Sporting Cyclist*. Wadley, a gentlemanly type who was always assumed at the Tour de France to be from the *Times* rather than a monthly with a minute specialist circulation, was complaining to Gayfer that he didn't feel as fit in his sixties as he had when younger.

'How do you mean?' asked Gayfer, who was always struggling with avoirdupois.

'Well,' said Wadley without irony, 'I can't just get on my bike and ride a hundred miles without feeling tired.'

Gayfer came close to choking on his tea.

Cycling opens blood vessels through and to your muscles. Blood carries in oxygen and sugar and carts away waste. The first makes you ride more effortlessly, the second stops you aching afterwards. Cycling also eats fat. It helps if you're modestly fit already, of course, but fitness is specific to the activity. You can be a wonderful ballroom dancer, or the regional blow-football champion but only some of that fitness transfers to cycling. You'll be ahead of the slobs but even they will catch up in the end.

If you've got doubts, visit your doctor. Luckily, cycling is a prolonged activity with no sudden peaks. Physical movements are limited by pedals and handlebars. The smoothness makes it a great heart and lungs activity, and not throwing yourself around makes it safer than being chased by a man with a hockey stick. Your doctor will be delighted. The *British Heart Journal* in 1991 said twenty miles a week cycling reduced the risk of coronary heart disease by 50 per cent. You could cycle to the surgery. The time-trial champion Louise Wilkinson once startled an ante-natal clinic in Norwich by asking where she could safely leave a racing bike.

Take it easy. Start with two or three miles and build up to five or ten if you're not already ready to ride further. Ride through back streets to a park. Feed the ducks, have a pot of tea and ride back. Cycle to a café and listen to Ned Miller sing 'From a Jack to a King'. Amble to a nearby village, or a beach. Set yourself a pleasing target. It could be a village church, friends in a neighbouring town, a loop past two windmills, or a spot with an intriguing name, like World's End or Gubblecote. It's up to you. I did once ride to Gubblecote, near Tring in Hertfordshire, just for its name. I found it was the last place in Britain to dunk a witch in the pond. Moreover, the museum down the road contained two fleas, one in male clothes, the other in female. The pond and fleas are still there.

Rule 2 *Start easily and ride only to enjoy yourself.*

Remember that you've got to get home. The humble mayfly might use less energy weight-for-weight than a cyclist, but mayflies live only a day. They're crotchety by lunchtime and by evening they're dead. There's a moral there.

Doctors will tell you that fitness comes from exercise that lasts at least 20 minutes at least three times a week. Riding to work is great for that. It can also save you time and money. The National Travel Survey in 1988 showed that 61 per cent of car journeys are less than five miles (8 km). And most British towns, while busy, are still civilized. You might draw the line at crossing central London, but the capital isn't the rest of Britain. Peterborough, Nottingham, Norwich and some other towns have gone out of their way to encourage cyclists with cycle lanes or quiet routes.

I enjoy cycling to work. I can go so many different ways and along alleyways and farm tracks. I like that smug feeling of doing something with the morning. I haven't just gone from home to work. I also – and this might sound daft, but it's a big thing – know which way the wind is blowing. I taunt colleagues who think they live an outdoor life because they cross the firm's car park each morning. The superiority keeps me going until lunchtime.

Wear working clothes if it's only a few miles. Otherwise, take shirts, blouses, skirts, shoes or whatever on the first day and cycle in there-after. You'll feel strange at first, changing in the loo, but we live in healthy times and people cycling or running no longer make bosses swoon. A relative of mine once told his deputy, an accountant, that he could cycle to work only if he arrived early and unseen. Now employ-ers want their workers healthy – it's in their interests as well – and the more enterprising can be coaxed into providing a shower.

The rest of the staff might copy you. I worked on the *Evening Telegraph* in Peterborough and cycled 23 miles each way. That's a long way even for a committed cyclist, but the journey became a mantra to start and close the working day. I waved to crop-pickers in the Fen fields, and became the subject of witty suggestions from women farm-workers carried past in old Transits. It took an hour and a half each way so I had three hours in the open, free of charge . . . plus the filthy jokes.

The 'free of charge' appealed to the staff. They calculated how much I saved on fares and car maintenance, and they began riding as well. They often came only three or four miles around the city's beautiful cycleways (and the undersized deputy news editor was once famously crowned by a sugar beet falling from a lorry on its way to the neigh-bouring processing factory) but numbers grew so large that the company decided against doing away with the bike sheds and built better ones instead.

My greatest triumph was with a colleague who insisted she couldn't balance. I told her of David E.H. Jones, who tried in the 1970s to make an unridable bike. He reversed the forks to stop the castor action, made the front wheel move in the opposite direction to the handlebars, and he stopped the wheels acting as gyroscopes. But he could always balance. He failed only when he locked the steering solid. My colleague did start riding – not every day, and certainly not far, but she did start. I tell myself she felt better for it. Once you've beaten a stiff breeze or shower, nothing at work is going to bother you.

> **Rule 3** *Look at your bike last thing at night; discover a slow puncture then, not in the morning when you're in a hurry.*

Gears and Pedalling

If you've got a bike with only one gear, you're stuck with what you've got. But that's a rare machine these days, so use the gears sensibly. The temptation is to slog against the pedals, using force rather than niftiness. Don't. If in doubt, pedal slightly faster than seems right rather than more slowly. Put the ball of your foot on the pedal, and never the arch, and turn the pedals round briskly. If in doubt, change down a gear. You can't always get the gear you want, especially with widely spaced hub gears, so compromise is needed. But the principle holds that light pedalling makes you fitter faster – and you ache less afterwards.

Brisk pedalling is a skill, which is why lumbering at the pedals seems easier at first. But it soon comes. The reason you use the ball of your foot rather than the arch is to employ another lever – the ankle – to spread the load of pedalling further. If you want to look like a duck on a bike, carry on pedalling underneath the arches.

Short Cuts and Detours

Most of my rides have been through open country but it hasn't always been so. For years I commuted from north to central London, including a spell to *Cycling's* office in Fleet Street. I soon realized the bus route wasn't best. It stuck to main roads because side roads were narrow with parked cars; entering and leaving depended on getting across stationary traffic. I cut through back streets, around parks and industrial estates. I knew the local curiosities: strange monuments in parks, pubs with bizarre names. I gained nodding acquaintance with greengrocers unloading apples and policemen having ciggies in doorways. It became a point of honour to find another short cut. It added to the fun. I looked for runs of suburban streets and alleyways. And once or twice in midsummer I rode out in a different direction and took a loop home through Burnham Beeches north of Slough by way of a drink in Amersham.

I wasn't alone. Johnny Helms was always pushed for time on his journey to ICI in Runcorn. But the journey back could take its own pace. At times he'd go out of his way to enjoy the journey . . .

'Yes sir?' said the landlord of the Spinner and Bergamot.

'A pint of bitter, please.' I watched with pleasurable anticipation as the liquid swirled and frothed into the glass tankard and then settled into a clear amber liquid that sparkled in the sunlight streaming through the open windows. It tasted as good as it looked and I emptied half the tankard in one long, slow, satisfying draught.

'Aaaaaah . . . that was good.'

'You're cycling, sir?'

'Yes, I'm just on the way home from work.'

'And where do you work?'

'Runcorn.'

'That's a long way on a bicycle.' (It is, in fact, about 12 miles.)

'And where do you live?'

'Widnes.'

The landlord opened his mouth and then shut it again. He appeared to be confused. Widnes is one mile north of Runcorn, across the river Mersey. The Spinner and Bergamot lies well to the east of both.

'You're not lost, sir?' A reasonable question from anyone who thinks that travelling is just getting from A to B, or Runcorn to Widnes.

'No, I often come this way.' Or through Delamere Forest. Or through the serenely quiet villages of Daresbury and Hatton. I use about twenty different routes to and from work. The shortest is five miles and the longest about forty. The Spinner and Bergamot is on the 33-mile route.

Beware minor enthusiasms. Some years ago a group of friends met in London to ride to Brighton. They did it again and brought a few friends. Over a few years, the ride became an institution akin to (but easier than, having done both) the London Marathon. There are now 40,000 on the London–Brighton, entertained by jugglers, street theatre and the inevitable accidents of letting loose a lot of people whose skill, enthusiasm and brakes aren't always up to the occasion. The police now beg only registered riders to take part, although it's hard to see what they can do about it.

Clothing

And I'll give you another tip here: think about what you wear. In pictures of the 1940s, everybody wears coat and hat and carries gloves. It was no colder, so the answer is that folk spent more time outdoors. They walked to the station or bus-stop, or all the way to work. They lived without central heating and worked with one small radiator.

Nothing beats specialist cycling clothing. (The advertising isn't compulsory.)

Cycling clothing can be practical without being garish. Jackets and sleeves are longer than usual, and the collar is higher. The tracksuit bottoms are cut tight round the legs but looser elsewhere to make you comfortable in the saddle. The shoes, more like trainers than racing shoes, have a sole flexible enough for walking but with a recessed pedal clip for cycling.

Now we move from central heating to a garage, to a car with a heater, to a well-warmed office.

Drivers don't care if it rains, and pedestrians rarely go more than 4mph but a cyclist can move at 20mph downhill with no effort, which brings the temperature down markedly. It might be 50°F but ride into a 15mph headwind at 10mph and the air is down to freezing. It doesn't *feel* that way – look at a bus queue and you'll notice that although you're in your own private Arctic, you're warm from pedalling while they, in air that's warmer, are freezing. If that doesn't bring on smugness, nothing will.

But you'll only feel self-satisfied if you put on an extra layer, maybe two or three. On a summer's day, you need no more than a pedestrian does. A shirt or blouse and a pair of shorts are fine. But the faster you ride, the more you need. That's why cyclists on the way to the beach look overdressed. You need an extra layer because you're cutting

Never wander far without waterproofs – either something fancy, or something traditional like this lightweight cape and cheap plastic hat . . .

. . . which you can roll up into a small bundle and strap under your saddle; you'd never get expensive waterproofs this tiny.

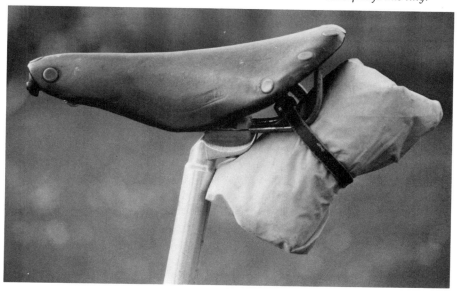

through air. If you forget it, you'll sweat, cool down in the breeze, use energy to get warm again, sweat more in the process and so on in a wet-chill cycle. You might also need gloves – lined nylon ski mitts are not just strong and warm, they're also cut in the right shape – and perhaps also a woollen hat to pull down over your ears.

> **Rule 4** *Wear more than you'd think, and take an extra jumper and something for the rain.*

Better still, buy specialist cycling clothes. The tops are longer and the trousers higher, so your back's covered. The sleeves also cover your wrists as you reach for the handlebars. On short rides and in good weather you need nothing special, but why give up cycling just because it's raining or less than perfectly sunny?

Harassment

Oh yes . . . one more thing. You might feel self-conscious. Bikes are big things and you're up there with the van drivers, higher than families in their cars. And while the world remains amicable, polite and easy-going, there are nevertheless people sufficiently frustrated by your freedom to ride past them to want to shout things. As long ago as 1890, an irate letter to the *Daily Cyclist* (yes, I was also surprised) protested: 'Almost every day I receive comments because I am a woman on a bicycle. . . . Men save their oppressive comments for the numerous occasions when traffic noise will ensure that only you will hear what they say, or for when, after dark or on quiet streets, there is no one else around. . . . Is this why most male cyclists remain blissfully unaware of what goes on?'

Well, being a bloke I can't really say. It happens (to me, anyway) infrequently and the girls in the back of the Wisbech Transits enjoyably pushed up the average. Mostly you can't hear. And anyway, what the hell, when you're out there and he's in there with his half-eaten sandwiches, a boss on the phone complaining that he's behind with the sales returns, and nothing on the radio but *Woman's Hour*?

Sometimes it's just plain funny. The Brecon Beacons are an uphill sort of a place and climbs go further than most might wish. I was struggling up one on a warm Easter Sunday with a posse of flies that had made it to altitude by buzzing around my brow. I was enjoying the self-imposed misery in the way that monks feel good about sackcloth.

And I was taking my superiority seriously. Two hundred metres from the top, the window opened in a car straining by only a little faster and a big round face stuck itself out of the window. With a Halloween smile and mock-sympathetic intonations, it said in a sing-song: 'Come on, bhoyo . . . *lag-ging* a bit aren't you?' I burst out laughing and had to push the bike the rest of the way to the top. I found him still enjoying his joke and emptying a Thermos.

Refreshments

The growth of fast roads and a disinclination to stop has led a lot of motorists – me included, I suppose – to kill off the Old Country Café. The only place to stop in most areas outside pub hours is a Little Chef or a Happy Eater. Nostalgia lends a hue to old cafés, but the more I think about them, the more I decide that many were closed not by trade but by sanitation inspectors.

Nevertheless, two opposing factors remain: you have to eat and drink, and there are fewer places of character in which to do it. Which

Vital for more than a few miles – an alloy cage to carry a bottle of drink. The plastic tongue is to hold the bottle secure and guide it into the rack as you ride.

leaves pubs. Pubs have replaced the country café. Publicans make more from food than beer. They have done wonders for cycling, especially on Sundays. I shouldn't have to add (although I will, because otherwise I'll get letters) that although cyclists can't be breath-tested, the rules of drink–driving nevertheless apply. You're more likely to injure yourself than someone else by drinking too much, and even a little alcohol makes your legs leaden. So, caution. The landlord makes more profit from coffee and soft drinks. He'd rather you got home safely and returned for another drink.

> **Rule 5** *Always carry a drink if you're cycling for more than half an hour, and never skip a meal if you're out for a morning or longer.*

The most enthusiastic followers of this rule are the sections, or local groups, of the CTC. The rounded bottoms of the, er, more relaxed members are proof that it also stands for Coffee, Tea and Cakes.

Eat and drink before you feel hungry or thirsty. By the time the symptoms appear, it's too late. This isn't a gluttons' charter (cycling uses 300 to 800 calories an hour, but you'd use 150 just wandering around the house anyway) but overestimating your fitness and under-doing the refuelling leads to Hades rather than heaven.

I once persuaded lads rather sportier than I was to join me on a hostelling trip to a hamlet in Suffolk called Nedging Tye. I liked the name. It was midwinter and we bowled out through Hertfordshire until, close on darkness and knackered to the point of trance, I sent them on ahead, promising that somehow I'd join them later.

I sat in the doorway of Budgen's, eating fig rolls. I looked like one of those poor sods slumped in Flanders with his tin hat balanced on his rifle. I persuaded Sudbury police to look after my bike, curled my arm around my luggage, and began hitching to Nedging Tye. I got a lift to Lavenham. And there I was stuck. I had too little money for a hotel. It was bitterly cold. At 10pm, I pulled coconut matting into a cor-ner of the church doorway, put on my rain-cape for warmth and went to sleep with my head on my bag.

I woke stiff, my cape frost-rigid. What disturbed me were the high heels of a country lady approaching to turn on the heaters for morn-ing service. She put me against the pinging radiators as the first warmth trickled into them. And then in slippers – because cycling shoes are difficult for walking – I trudged 7 miles into Sudbury for my bike and caught the train home. The lads said later that it had ruined their weekend.

2

Ho for the Open Road

The publishing people at Shell bring out guides to the countryside – Roman roads or villages or the coastline, and so on. I plan to write the *Shell Guide to the Most Boring Roads of Britain*. It will feature the M11. The M11 is the dullest highway in the universe. It will become a Listed Monument, a tribute to tedium. It doesn't quite go to London, it doesn't quite go to Cambridge. It rolls through fields which have no more trees and hedges than Stansted airport, which it also doesn't quite go to. Even so, every so often, I spot cyclists trying to complete its length. That they're American I can see from their mirrors, crash helmets, bright red luggage, and their swaying whip aerials with pennants on top. Motorists gesture furiously, and, being Americans and therefore friendly, they wave back. 'Hi, fella!'

It's not riding on the hard shoulder of the M11 that bothers me. After all, the speed limit's no different and the side-strip is wider than on a conventional road. No, why I'd beat them about their plastic helmets is that they, Americans or not, haven't worked out that Britain's got the greatest density of quiet lanes, byways and tracks in the world. There are 1,768 miles of unclassified roads in Suffolk alone, 1,826 miles in Somerset, and so it goes on. As my fist descends rhythmically on their heads, I will chant: 'Listen, you numbskulls, even the most pot-holed and miserable lane in the whole land is more pleasant than a bleak motorway in Essex.' After that I would drive to the next emergency telephone and ask the police not to prosecute, because any cyclist on the M11 has served sentence enough.

Rule 6 *Choose the smallest road.*

You'll disappear into that Real Britain that lesser folk see only from by-passes or the car park listed in a 'Get To Know Real Britain' supplement of the *Sunday Times*. When they get there, hot and bothered and desperate for the loo, you'll sail by. In fact, on a bike you're a participant rather than an observer, so you'll be part of the Real Britain that the others have come to see. It's a curious notion. Ramblers must feel it, too.

I confess I'm stuck on how to explain that a ride is more than riding a bike. Like those Russian dolls, there's more hidden beneath the obvious. It's not just the scenery (from Wagnerian Highlands to the Vaughan Williams gentleness of Cambridgeshire); it's not the exercise (becalmed or storm-tossed). It's . . . it's . . . well, I don't know, except that it's pretty special and it changes every time.

In October 1992 *CT&C* (*Cycle Touring & Campaigning*, the CTC magazine) printed this lovely letter. May it be as much fun for you. You don't, by the way, have to succumb to gravity quite so often.

'How's this for cycling memories of a teenager's youth-hostelling trip, 21 years ago? First postcard – Monday: "Dear Dom and Mad, We are having a nice time but Christine and me are minus mudguards due to a pile-up where Jill was cut-up, Suzanne put her brakes on suddenly, I went into her and fell on the bank. Christine piled up on the road and Kate came off on the road and grazed her sunburn, but we are still in one piece and everybody shouts 'stopping' when they stop now. Anyway I kept the reflector and stays and half of it is still there. Love, M."

'Second postcard – Wednesday: "Dear Dom and Mad, We are having a nice time, I thought I'd write another card as the other one wasn't very cheerful. So far we've had six punctures, two broken mudguards, two people have been sick, one had sunstroke and slightly buckled but ridable wheel. We couldn't go swimming because it was cold and wet and they had a red flag out. We're enjoying ourselves immensely. Also we've opened the trapdoor in the dormitory to look in the blokes' dormitory. Oh, yes! And us three fell off, but I've told you about that already. By the way, we're going to the New Forest and the Isle of Wight next year. Love, M." '

'M', I gather, is still riding a bike. So am I.

Road Classifications

A benefit of being invaded by more orderly nations is that we've acquired an enthusiasm for numbering things and putting them in order. We grade everything from tracks to motorways.

Footpaths are for walkers. They're shown on the Ordnance Survey Landranger 1:50,000 map as ·······, in black if there's no right of way, red if there is. A lot exist only on the map as the Countryside Commission reckoned in 1989 that 25,000 of the 140,000 miles of foot-path, bridleway and byway in England and Wales are unusable. That's just 18 per cent, but the Commission said you had only a 2 per cent chance of completing a 10-mile journey by bridleway.

Footpaths are supposed to be 'wide enough for two men to pass without argument', but often the plough or undergrowth or field enlargements got there first. Technically this shouldn't matter, since you can't cycle on a footpath legally anyway (although you can push a bike). Path law is so vague that some people say no cyclist would be prosecuted for pedalling. The belief's grown with mountain-biking. But it misses the spirit. If cyclists expect landowners and ramblers not to object, logic says cyclists shouldn't raise an eyebrow if motorists begin driving on bridleways.

Bridleways are aristocratic footpaths, usually wider and more eas-ily spotted. They're often old cart roads, sometimes easily ridable. The CTC won the right to cycle on bridleways in 1968. Some of the most wonderful rides in Britain are along bridleways. They're shown as ------. At the same time the CTC tried to get access to footpaths as well, but the idea was rejected.

A road used as a public path – a **Rupp** – is a town hall bodge. Men in dull spectacles elevate bridleways to Rupps, which is a shame because anyone can drive a car transporter legally down a Rupp whereas the only traffic allowed on bridleways belongs to neighbour-ing landowners. The car transporter's unlikely but trail-riding motorcyclists are predictable. Rupps are ·--·--·--·. on the map.

Next is a rare thing called the **byway open to all traffic**. It's not worth explaining how it differs from a Rupp (oh, all right, I don't *know* how it differs, since there's nothing you can do on a byway that you can't also do on a Rupp). You'll know you're on one, though, when you find +·+·+·+·+· on the map.

Scots classify cycling as mechanical walking. You can cycle wherever you can walk. Ireland's never thought to define rights of way. Fortunately both have more countryside than people and so if you use your sense and avoid back gardens, or deer-stalking country in autumn, you're not likely to meet resistance. Surfaced roads (in Scotland, too) follow the same ascending pattern, often with the same unclear distinctions.

The OS shows C-roads in yellow, B-roads in orange-brown, and A-roads in red (with a thick black edge for dual carriageways). Motorways are pale blue and, until the OS widened them on the map, were frequently mistaken for canals. The consequences are delightful to imagine.

I'm not sure when this classification began. A between-the-wars map says it hasn't yet happened, and a Girl Guide annual of the late 1930s explains that it has. So some time between the two, a minister numbered all the main roads from London clockwise, starting with the A1 (to Edinburgh) and then moving through the A2 (Dover), A3 (Portsmouth), A4 (Bristol), A5 (Holyhead) and A6 (Manchester). He gave Scotland the A7, A8, and A9. The first major road from the A2 became the A20, the next the A21, and tributaries to those became the A201, the A210, and so on.

Lesser routes became B-roads. Then the minister decided there'd be C-roads. These have numbers repeated every few parishes. Signposts in Lincolnshire's Fens show numbers of C-roads, but it's always too windy to stop and ask why. The Fens, anyway, do eccentric things of their own; several signboards which anywhere else would be white were for years still 1950s yellow in Spalding.

Ireland's main roads are N or T, with signs changing from one to the other, and B-roads are L-roads. The six counties of the North, and the Isle of Man, follow the British mainland tradition but use the numbers again. There are too few roads on Jersey, Guernsey, the Scillies and the rest to be troubled.

Since then some A-roads have been demoted. Even the arterials haven't escaped: the A5 changes four times in its first 40 miles (64km) from London. There must be a reason, although traffic on the B sections is as heavy as on the A. So why? Perhaps people in Elstree and St Albans speak of little else. A B-road in Surrey can be busier than A-roads in Cumbria. Many Home Counties B-roads, especially south of London, enter one housing area only half a mile after the last. They might not connect conurbations, but the string of villages makes them busy routes with lights, kerbs, yellow lines, double white lines and all the trappings of a highway. And they are often driven accordingly.

On the other hand, anyone who last saw the A1 where it crossed the M25 in Hertfordshire would never recognize it north of Newcastle. This once six-lane highway has become safe to bowl hoops and gather chickens. You can stand some mornings by the sign that explains the ferry times to Lindisfarne and feel you've dropped into a Hovis advert.

So what do you do? You go for the best option. Avoid the North Devon coast road and you miss the views. The road around the south-west of the Isle of Wight has no cross-country route to replace it. And there are limited ways of crossing Snaefell on the Isle of Man, as the people who live there must regret during TT week.

The best C-roads are little wider than two cyclists side by side. They twist and add miles to your journey. What was it G.K. Chesterton wrote?

> Before the Romans came to Rye or out to Severn strode
> The rolling English drunkard made the rolling English road.

But C-roads are fun. They hide in cuttings, overhung by trees, and strewn by leaves, and they cross the cathedral openness of the Fens. You can cross Britain by nothing bigger than a B-road. You might cross the flow of traffic and the grain of the land, and you feel you've seen the whole country without having been anywhere (C-roads usually miss even medium-sized towns) but give me lanes every time. They're not favoured by people who replace wooden signposts with metal reflective ones. They see C-roads as feeders, so their signs instruct you off the lane and on to the through route. It's motorists they're after, to preserve the villages. But take no notice. It takes nerve to trust your map rather than signs, but you'll get a better ride and, occasionally, a shorter one as well. There are lanes south of Norwich which for mile after mile tell you you're going 90 degrees in the wrong direction. And so you are if you'd rather be on the Ipswich–Norwich main road. Similarly, there's a 15-mile cross-country route in southern Kent rarely wide enough to play hopscotch but which seldom deviates from a straight line by more than half a mile.

Getting There

Roads like those make cycling magical. Oh, there are days when the wind blows and the sun goes down early and your legs refuse to come to life. But think of the film *White Mischief*. The idle rich have filled their day with drink, fine food and promiscuity. As the sun sets over Kenya's parakeets and zebra, one character complains wearily: 'Oh God, yet *another* day in Paradise.' Of course, you've still got to *get* to Paradise. There's much to be said for living in the country, but most people don't. There are spiders there, and few all-night supermarkets, and no grainy French films in which the characters remove their clothes unexpectedly to slow music on an oboe.

You could ride there, of course. In medium-sized towns that's no problem. You can concoct a route through parks, canal banks and cycle routes. But central Birmingham, Manchester and Glasgow are different. The ride beyond the semi-country occupied by commuter villages and garden centres isn't just unpleasant, it's further than you wanted to ride in the first place. And so you think about going by train or car.

By Rail

An ecological voice says the train is cleaner, safer. You're not spoiling what you came to see. And you think you could spend all day with the wind behind you, getting out at one station and returning from another. Sunday work might slow or even stop the train, but Railways Are A Good Thing. Sadly, as Jerome K. Jerome pointed out in *Three Men on the Bummel*, 'this is an imperfect world of joy and sorrow mingled'. What you would like to happen rarely matches reality. British Rail has never made life simple for cyclists and the more paperwork it produces to say that it *is*, the more it makes sure that it's not.

We used to grumble when BR asked half as much again to take a bike where bulkier items, such as prams, went free. For cyclists seen as paupers because they weren't driving, paying the first-class fare to go by bike was breathtaking. So, on 1 June 1977, to mark the Queen's jubilee, we celebrated when BR dropped all charges. We didn't quite get to Easter 1898, when 50,000 cyclists left Waterloo station alone, or when the CTC chartered trains to take contented cyclists out of the suburbs but we did, according to BR, clog up the railways. Among the extra traffic were pin-stripers who saw not an incentive to use the railways – their season tickets already committed them to that – but a way to beat Tube and bus fares. Alarms rang and in came charges and restrictions. Almost monthly changes led the CTC magazine to headline stories with a weary 'BR – Again.'

Ten years after charges were dropped, and only a little less after they were reintroduced, *CT&C* wrote: 'The future is certainly not something to contemplate with any satisfaction. The present situation [in which trains take only limited numbers of bikes] is unacceptable to families or groups – ironically the users who stood to gain most from the 1977 free offer. . . . It may be significant that around a dozen stands at the recent Olympia cycle show included some sort of fold-down bike.' Folding bikes travelled, and still do, free of BR restrictions.

You *can* still get out of town, and some places are better than others. But what's possible at noon on Saturday in one direction isn't necessarily so on Tuesday in the other. Or it depends whether anyone got there before you, since some trains limit the number of bikes. Whole cross-country journeys by HST 125s have become impossible.

Sometimes bikes have to be booked, yet few country stations have ticket offices and even fewer travel agents understand train tickets. The nearest booking station might be the one you're trying to reach. BR staff themselves are confused. I've arrived at an East Anglian station for a train advertised as taking unbooked bikes, only to find a chalked message saying it didn't. There was no explanation: it just wasn't going to take bikes. All the documentation in the world is useless if they're not going to let you on.

When you do get aboard, label your bike with the destination or changing point of *that* train. The guard can then sort his luggage into the order of off-loading. Put nothing, and you'll find your bike hidden by mail bags. Never lock it in place. If the postmen can't move it, it doesn't stand a chance. Use elastic straps attached to the wire netting. Load the bike yourself (you'll have to anyway) and forget the days when Brunel ran the Great Western Railway and God was a shareholder and the guard's van was always at the back. It rarely is nowadays. Often there's more than one, but only one will be unlocked. Stand a third down the platform, towards where the train will pull in, and run your eye over the carriages until you spot a peaked cap. That's the guard.

Sprinter and other modern short trains have a luggage area at each end. The bike area in some is revealed by folding up a bench seat. You must hope it's not occupied by two fierce ladies searching the *Daily Express* for news that we've got India back. On trains covering longer distances, one area holds the tea-trolley. Unfortunately, you can't see from the outside which it is. Choose the wrong one while the trolley's out dispensing Fresh Brew and Sandwiches and you'll cause a traffic jam which can't be sorted out until the next stop.

I don't want to put you off travelling by train. Yours might be a contented line where the staff smile while watering flowerbeds. Praise them and let them know you welcome their service. But if it isn't and BR has ceased to be a service, complain not only to it – complaints are logged and their numbers published – but to the passengers' organization listed on noticeboards and to your MP (you after all pay for the railways, even after privatization, but your MP ultimately runs them).

And now a happy thought: the Metropolitan, District and Circle lines in London take bikes all weekend and on holidays, and from 10am to 4pm and after 7pm during the week. Even at half fare, this is a good option. The Metropolitan runs to rural Buckinghamshire. Check with London Underground (tel: 0171-222 1234, 24 hours).

And now you want another happy story to cheer you up? Right. . . . For all the aggravations, railways are sometimes on the side of the angels. Stranded in Antwerp with an unridable bike, I caught an all-station stopper only to be off-loaded several miles from my home in Belgium. Services from there would be by bus – but no, *mijnheer*, the bus couldn't take a bike. So what to do?

The stationmaster rang the signal box and ordered the halting of the imminent Trans-European Express from Brussels to Amsterdam. My predicament was explained and the bike was loaded. Bikes are never normally carried on TEE trains within the same country. Four stops up the line, this enormous train overhung the station at Kalmthout while a British cyclist and his busted bike were lowered to the platform. And then it pulled out again with several hundred mystified Dutchmen on board.

> **Rule 7** *Never give up on railways . . . but check with at least three people first.*

By Road

And so reluctantly you decide to drive. A van will take bikes upright and complete; a hatchback will take one, possibly two, with wheels removed. Use an old blanket to stop one bike scratching another. The bikes can't be stolen if you leave the car, which they can if you put them outside. Racing cyclists for years turned their bikes upside down and strapped the handlebars and saddles to a conventional roof-rack. The whole lot was made to look safer with elastic guy-ropes. It took nerve, but I don't know anybody who lost a bike. If you decide to copy them, remember to place sponge between the saddle and the rack; if you don't, the saddle will dent or, worse, tear. The damage might be perceptible only long-term; if you've got a plastic saddle covered with chamois or some other padding, the surface can become detached from the base and wrinkle just enough that you feel it after fifty miles or so.

You can just about fiddle four bikes on to a decent rack, although three are simpler. Do it by alternating bikes, so that saddles sit beside handlebars. Dropped handlebars are easier than straight ones. Use roller-buckle straps of the sort used in pedals to fasten the fixing points. There's nothing better. I'd rather fix my bike that way than with one of those half-and-half rack attachments that have a plastic scoop for the saddle and clamps for the handlebars. I've never made one work. Buy a specialist rack. It holds the bike securely, upright or inverted, sometimes with one wheel removed, sometimes not. It's not cheap but nothing's better.

Remember, once you've put the bike up there, that it's still there. You'll know when you're driving around from the way other drivers gawp at it. It's harder travelling more slowly. I know that to my cost. I once rode 80 miles into a headwind to the north Norfolk town of Hunstanton, where my car had been left for me in a seafront car park. I was exhausted when I got there and I didn't notice that the car park entrance included a hanging horizontal bar, like a loading gauge, to stop lorries stopping there. The car, without the bike, had entered easily. On the return journey, though, grateful I was no longer pedalling into that wind, I drove the bike straight into the bar and wrecked the front wheel and forks. You have been warned.

There are also racks to hang over the back of the car, often supported by a towing point. Many people use them, but they give me doubts. For one, bikes obscure the rear view. They also hide the brake lights. And, third, they're a sharp obstruction to anyone who piles into you. There's also the point that factories make their cars as smooth and aerodynamic as possible, and there are legal limits to what you can hang outside them. I've heard of drivers being stopped with these racks but never of being prosecuted. Ask the makers for their assurance. Check, too, that the rack fits your car perfectly, otherwise both attachment and bikes will sway as you drive.

3

The Glory of Mud

You know what I like about riding cross-country? It's the freedom and adventure, and that fear that any moment I'll fall into a stream. But most of all, it's the mud-pies sensation. I know my bike's going to drip slime and leaves all the way home and we'll both need hosing down afterwards – and that's fine by me. I tell people it's only a wish to get closer to nature, but it's not. That's the respectable argument. Oh sure, I genuinely do like being closer to nature, but I also love going back to the days when it was forgivable to splash in puddles with my wellingtons. I spend all day forgetting that I'm grown up. I ride where my father said I couldn't, and I get that tingly feeling that I'm going to cop it when I get home. And it's not just me, because if it were, ramblers would stick to pavements and yachtsmen would sail on reservoirs. And where's the excitement in that?

It's called off-road riding these days, but it's had lots of names, because it's not new. High on a crossing in Wales is a memorial to a writer called Wayfarer. He was the Alfred Wainwright of the years after the First World War, although for cyclists rather than walkers. He became a celebrity in 1919 after he hauled his bike through the snow over the Berwyn Mountains and got back to write an article for *Cycling*. He's always been known as Wayfarer because it was the custom of the day to use a pen-name rather than style himself W. Robinson.

He wasn't the first to discover that cycling through mud is fun. It's done wonders for cycling and the bike industry, and some say it's the way that *all* leisure cycling will be. Who can blame them? Cars trebled in the ten years after the war and bike sales fell below 500,000 a year. There were still only 700,000, to a much increased population, in 1972. Then came the 1980s boom, with 2,150,000 sales in 1983, and just as that was dying so in came the mountain bike to make cycling acceptable and cross social barriers. Eight out of ten bikes are now for adults. Sales still nudge two million a year. I don't suppose more than a fraction ever leave hard roads, but they could. The man who devised ads for the Saracen factory in the Midlands said pictures of riders scaling mountains and being boiled by cannibals were saying 'I might not *want* to ride across deserts and wildernesses on this bike, *but I could do it if I wanted to.'* So give it a go. There are very few cannibals in the Home Counties.

Why ride across mud, stone and heath? Well, the roads have become busier. Decades ago, an H.G. Wells character grumbled: 'The world has thrown up a new type of gentleman altogether, a gentleman of the most ungentlemanly type, a gentleman in dusty oilskins and motor goggles and a wonderful cap, a stink-making gentleman, a swift, high-class badger, who fled perpetually along high roads from the dust and stink he perpetually made.'

These were motorcyclists, but we get the picture. You can see why he worried; of all those injured or killed on the road in 1936, 31 per cent were cyclists. In 1937 Nottinghamshire police called for speeding motorists to be flogged. I imagine both drivers and chief constables have since become better tempered, but the wish to escape from traffic is stronger than ever.

More of Britain is being built on – whole new towns and villages now rather than small estates. Worcestershire has lost 30 per cent of its ancient woodlands, half its pools, 95 per cent of the marshes and bogs, 99 per cent of pastures, and 2,500 miles of hedge since the war. Seven per cent of Britain is wooded, but 80 per cent of that is commercial conifers. The more we lose, the greater is the wish to enjoy what remains.

You need only three things: a bike that won't jam with mud, sensible clothes, and an understanding of the country and those who share it. Any bike will do in dry weather and a true mountain bike with enormous clearances and knobbly tyres will go anywhere a tank could manage. Mud drives you mad if your mudguards are too close to the tyres. Scooping it out with a stick is what puts most people off. It's also why many mountain bikes have no mudguards, although you trade keeping going for mud up your back and legs.

Technique

Cross-country cycling is harder than road cycling. Surfaces are uneven and cloying; you'll waste energy keeping upright or struggling in dips and soft spots. Low gears are essential – derailleur gears for choice, although the lowest hub gear should see you through all but the worst. Go gently. Sometimes the only place to fall is against a tree, down a ditch or into barbed wire. Use a gear low enough to plough through wet mud but not so low that the wheels spin. Keep your weight steady across the saddle and handlebars; don't get out of the saddle to press on the pedals because you'll lose control. Move forward on the saddle as the going gets harder, back as it eases. And remember that your brakes work nowhere as well as on a dry road and that traction under your tyres is much reduced.

If you can let the bike rip down hill, do it with the cranks horizontal, not vertically as you would on the road. Put your weight on both pedals and stand just clear of the saddle. But never do it unless you're convinced you'll get to the bottom without interruption. Use the back brake more than on the road; you can control a back-wheel skid easily on mud but it feels startling on the road.

Given time and a willingness to enjoy yourself, off-road riding is wonderful. Cycling on the road, even a circular route, always has the feeling of needing to get somewhere. But on mud, the fun is the doing. Don't expect to go much faster than you could have walked it.

Rights of Way

Cross-country cycling varies as much as the country you cross. Mastiles Lane is a stony path wandering across north Yorkshire; chalk tracks along the Wiltshire dales are treacherous in rain; Cumbrian and Northumbrian paths are lonely places of springy turf and deep bog trod more by sheep than men. But wherever you are, watch the weather. Mist falls rapidly on Dartmoor, rivers torrent within moments in the Highlands, and snow falls on the Peaks while the valleys are in sun. Wear warm clothing and have more handy. Take food and drink. In wild country, take a whistle, a plastic bag to sleep, and food. Turn back if you're in doubt.

So where do you ride? Let's re-track. In England and Wales, you can ride any path classified from bridleway upwards. You can also push your bike on a footpath. Give way to ramblers and horses. Signs that trespassers will be prosecuted or that the path is private can be ignored. The land beside it will be private but not the path.

Where the right goes is harder to prove. Bridleways are fairly clear, but footpaths run from field to field, and fields change shape. More, hedges aren't shown on Landranger maps and are often out of date on the impractical but larger Pathfinder maps. The definitive route is at county hall, but that's of little use when confronted by a hostile landowner. Those were once more numerous than they are now. They emerged from their Land Rovers with heavy sticks and even shotguns to warn what they saw as trespassers off what they considered *their* paths. Since then landowners have become more tolerant, better advised. You can't be turned off a right of way and you should insist politely that this is the case – provided you are on the right path.

A path is not simply a route from one point to another. It exists precisely and many run through crops. It might seem reasonable to skirt a field to oblige the farmer, but it's then that you're trespassing (trespass is damage to other people's land) and not when you flatten the crops. Leaving the path might cause no more damage than squashed grass, but it could scare lambing sheep or let cattle stray. A farmer who ploughs a path, or sows it, must reinstate it or pay a penalty (rarely enforced). A right of way ceases if the land disappears. If the cliff edge topples, the path vanishes with it.

Once a route had to be travelled each year to remain legal passage. Ancient records would disappear as farmers fought to close their land; ageing villagers were dragged out to scour their memories. Magistrates could close a path that had existed for a thousand years, and landowners were better represented in the magisterial classes than your ordinary cyclist or rambler. The 1949 National Parks and Access to the Countryside Acts ended all that. Landowners now have to maintain not only the path but also ensure your safety. Some argue that warning of a dangerous bull – or perhaps any bull, since the sign's a warning – is acknowledgement of a deliberate hazard.

Even horses can provide a moment's excitement. The *Art and Pastime of Cycling* in the nineteenth century advised: 'Care should be taken by the cyclist not to startle any horse by passing at a high rate of speed, and upon meeting one which shows signs of restiveness he should ride slowly, and as far away as the width of the road permits, and should even stop if requested to do so by the driver.

'In most cases, though, it is better to proceed slowly and speak soothingly to the horse, as a sudden dismount when close at hand will startle more than anything else. The ground in front of a horse should not be taken until the rider is at least ten yards ahead. Horses standing by the roadside, unattended, should be approached with exceptional caution.'

Another drawback you'll face will wear a waxed jacket, large boots and a superior smirk. You'll be out in the rain, struggling through his wheel ruts, while he spins muddily past in his Japanese estate wagon. The damage these people did in 1994 cost Berkshire alone £150,000 to put right, and I don't suppose that was for anything but the worst ruts.

Cross men from Berkshire's footpaths department met colleagues from neighbouring counties; their view was that unless the four-wheel-drive squad regulated themselves, they'd do it for them. Which would be no bad thing. Or, it would be, if cyclists weren't getting caught by the ricochet. Elizabeth Still, an upset Berkshire lady, said: 'Drivers are legally entitled to use these public green paths and roads and we have relied on their voluntary co-operation to use them sensibly.' She's fed up with puddles over her wellingtons.

The same pressure is now coming to cyclists. You don't get the noise and you get a very inferior wheel rut from a mountain bike, but while walkers feel obliged to get out of the way of Land Rover drivers, galloping horsemen and cyclists alike, it's the cyclists who pass slowly enough to attract abuse. You can complain about a car driver but he can't hear you. A cyclist, on the other hand, can be felled like the blades on their penny-farthings, and for much the same reason – being irritating merely by being there.

This might be unfair. It *is* unfair if you're behaving yourself and saying 'Good morning' and letting the ramblers pass. But we have sinners in our midst. Alan Harlow, the director of the CTC, has warned that unless extreme mountain bikers in particular show more responsibility, they risk losing the right which took the CTC decades to win – to cycle on bridleways in the first place. It might seem good fun – oh all right, it *is* good fun – to ride light-headedly fast along a path knowing you're unlikely to be hurt if you fall, but you do nobody any favours by scattering middle-aged ladies in windcheaters and knitted hats as you pass. One day you will fall foul of a man with a walking stick. Your pancake into the slime will strike him as very amusing. And me, too, actually.

Walkers frequently have dogs. The only time that dogs are predictable is on country paths. It brings a contentment, all that rooting in hedgerows. But dogs on the open road are never as predictable. They lie in wait. Just as you think the sleepy lump by the road hasn't the energy, it becomes a fireball of aggression, racing across the road, snapping at your ankles. Loud noises are called for – and generous threats. The writer Richard Ballantine (*Richard's Bicycle Book*) once urged still more:

'Ram your pump down the dog's throat,' he triumphed. 'In any event, don't run, cower, or cover up, because the dog will only chew you to ribbons. *Attack* . . . breaking the dog's ribs or crushing its head with a rock. If worst comes to worst, ram your entire arm down his throat. He will choke and die. Better your arm than your throat.'

This took the RSPCA rather by surprise and Ballantine, a gentle and thoughtful man – 'I like dogs very much' – received the odd letter or two. I have had the occasional tussle with a dog, but never on so gory a scale. I've been seriously worried half a dozen times in twenty-five years but never bitten. Ballantine refused to remove it from later editions, although the advice that 'any small dog can simply be hoisted up by the legs and his brains dashed out' became the calmer 'a small dog can be scooped up by the rear legs and heaved away'.

I've never cracked a dog across the nose with a pump, although lord knows I've tried – which is as well because, regardless of the dog's opinion, pumps are expensive. Ballantine says 8 per cent of cycling accidents in his native USA are caused by dogs. American dogs, like Americans themselves, are clearly more given to violence. Either that or American cyclists have inferior pumps.

Finally, if you like your off-road adventure with mod-cons, there are paths, privately owned, on which you're welcome to ride. The Forestry Commission has two million acres and lets cyclists on its paths on the understanding that it's a privilege and not a right. Forest Enterprise, the part of the commission which owns the woods, got the message from Whitehall in 1994 that it must be more commercial. That means selling land, although the government says rules will protect public access. We must wait and see.

There are 2,000 miles of paths alongside canals and rivers and about half are available to cyclists. British Waterways will send you information for £5 and thereafter permits, which once cost several pounds a time, will be free. The address is British Waterways Customer Services, Willow Grange, Church Road, Watford WD1 3QA (tel.: 01923-226422). Signs are going up on paths closed to cyclists, usually because the surface is too poor and easily churned or, conversely, so good that cyclists would travel too fast for the safety of anglers and walkers.

There are more routes dedicated to walkers and cyclists every year. Sustrans (for Sustainable Transport) has been pricking the conscience of councils since 1979 to persuade them to pay for the conversion of railway beds and other routes. It makes paths just wide enough for cycling and walking through woods, parks and, it has to be said, the occasional industrial area. Gradients are trimmed and embankments and cuttings built. Other people have been working on similar schemes, so that you can pedal through the Peaks on the Tissington Trail, or along the banks of the lower Thames, where another project exists to link Berkshire with Essex. And then there are projects to build

1,000 miles of cycleways in the capital, and routes which already connect York with Selby and Bristol with Bath . . . and so it goes on.

The best way to learn about not only cycleways but routes around Britain (and the rest of the world) is to consult the CTC. Its headquarters in Godalming, Surrey, are chocker with everything from where to get your bottom bracket fixed near Barnstaple to how to ride safely between Delhi and Calcutta. The touring department answers 25,000 questions a year. The address is Cotterell House, 69 Meadrow, Godalming GU7 3HS (tel.: 01483-417217; fax: 01483-426994).

Other useful information comes from the Byways and Bridleways Trust at 9 Queen Anne's Gate, London SW1H 9BY; the Countryside Commission, at John Dower House, Crescent Place, Cheltenham GL50 3RA; Scottish Natural Heritage, Battleby, Redgorton, Perth PH1 3EW; the Open Spaces Society of 25a Bell Street, Henley RG9 2BA; and the Scottish Rights of Way Society, at 28 Rutland Avenue, Edinburgh EH1 2BW.

4

Step this Way . . .

My first map was of Dorset. It showed me how to get to Litton Cheney youth hostel, an old cheese factory with sloping floors and a stream to be crossed for the lavatory. The warden asked me to choose between tuning a piano and grooming his cat to defray expenses. I tuned the piano, no worse than anyone who'd preceded me, and certainly no better since all I had were bicycle spanners. Being ill-equipped always means a bodge – as subsequent pianists discovered. It's the same with maps. The only people interested in byways and paths and whether the land goes up or down are cyclists and ramblers. Motorists' maps from petrol stations are no use at all. Every so often someone tries to replace the Bartholomew half-inch edition which navigated me to Dorset but which has long been abandoned. *CT&C* lists another publisher every so often and the CTC shop stocks its maps, but they never get into general use.

Until someone finds something better, the only candidate is the Ordnance Survey Landranger. Its problem is that, for all its clarity and detail, it covers only 25 miles by 25. So if you live on the corner of one of the 204 sheets, you carry four on even a short ride. Embark on a weekend or longer and you've got an entire library in your panniers. It costs more than £500 to buy the whole set.

Barts was famously inaccurate at times (early editions proclaimed something like 'Mapped in co-operation with the CTC' and later Barts appealed for anyone who discovered mistakes to write in, and many sections of the CTC appointed map revision officers). Its white roads could be anything from little less than a B-road to an invisible field path, but it had a lovable quality and only 62 sheets. Half-inch and, later, five-eighths of an inch to the mile (or 1cm to a kilometre) was ideal. Even the OS had a half-inch map, which it kept until 1961, when it 'reluctantly decided to abandon' it because 'the commercial sector' – presumably Barts – was already established there. But Barts Leisure Series at 1:100,000 covers only popular touring areas and the mapping's often old. So the Landranger OS map it is.

Its scale is 1:50,000, or two centimetres to a kilometre. The Survey

There's no shortage of good maps – the trick is to get one of the right scale and the right amount of detail.

admits in its official history that metrication of the old one-inch map was 'a cause for some nervousness'. It had produced them since at least 1795, including a survey of Kent 'in conjunction with Mr Gardner, from which a very fine Map has been produced, containing all that part of the country, which, from its proximity to the coast, may in the process of time, become the seat of military operations'.

The post-war Seventh Series map was the last at an inch to the mile (1:63,360). In 1965 Prime Minister Harold Wilson declared, as part of his 'white heat of technology', that Britain would go metric. The Ordnance Survey responded by magnifying the one-inch, which was selling nearly a million and a half copies a year in 1966, to the slightly larger two centimetres to a kilometre. It dropped some of the detail at the same time; the Survey denies this, but it's wrong – apart from anything else, the symbols which showed whether a wood was coniferous or deciduous disappeared. On the new larger scale, the enlarged maps had a thin look. Roads became ugly, overlarge and clumsy. The Survey says that 'naturally there was criticism', although much was nostalgia at losing the one-inch. True, the one-inch was somewhat more attractive.

The truth is that the first metric edition was being replaced even as the first sheets of the old one were being printed (1974), and it had been superseded by the time (1976) it was complete. The current map is a great improvement and widely recognized as one of the clearest in the world. It doesn't have the detail of the continental Michelin maps, but it does have astonishing clarity and a logic of symbols, which Michelin doesn't. It also has contour lines. Close your eyes almost shut and the lines stand out. Barts used a different colour for each altitude, but since a less than warming experience with height shading on one-inch maps in 1935, the OS has been more cautious and prefers orange-brown lines to link points of equal height. Hills are therefore shown by concentric meandering rings and, unless they're jammed together, it takes a perceptive eye to spot them.

Perhaps a lot of people rang in to point this out. The OS got the message and combined colour shading and contours on its Tourist series. It brought back an inch to the mile for hilly or at least rolling areas such as the Cotswolds, Exmoor, Dartmoor, New Forest, Peak District, North York Moors, Loch Lomond, Trossachs, Ben Nevis and Glencoe. Then it brought out a map for the Norfolk Broads, which has no hills at all, and went back to metrication.

They're good maps, if strong on labelling steam museums, theme parks and large car parks more prominently than youth hostels, remote pubs and bridleways. Unfortunately neither they nor the conventional maps are cheap. The OS is a government agency told to cover its costs and better. It was trying to do that as long ago as 1913 when it took on a test case involving 'Rowe's New Road Map for Cyclists and Motorists'. Mr Rowe had decided to do away with almost all the costs of map-making by simply photo-copying the Ordnance Survey and selling his maps for threepence, somewhat less than the original. The OS has since become even keener on covering its costs and the prices change so fast that they're now attached to the map by sticker rather than being printed.

Small-scale maps are little use on the road, but they're fine for planning. Both Barts and the OS have plans of several counties at a time. The OS Travelmaster is five kilometres to a centimetre (1:250,000) and

Straßen - Bahnlinien / Roads - Railways

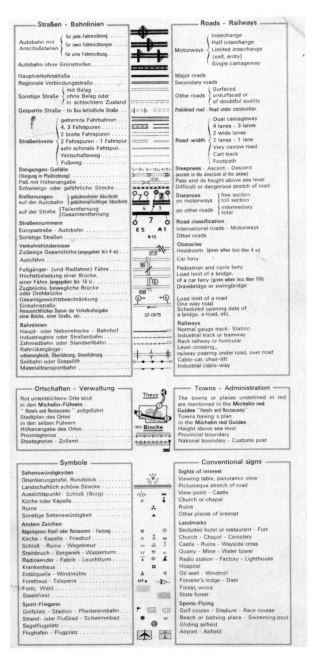

Straßen - Bahnlinien	Roads - Railways
Autobahn mit Anschußstellen: für jede Fahrtrichtung / für zwei Fahrtrichtungen / für eine Fahrtrichtung	Motorways: Interchange / Half interchange / Limited interchange / (exit, entry) / Single carriageway
Autobahn ohne Grünstreifen	
Hauptverkehrsstraße	Major roads
Regionale Verbindungsstraße	Secondary roads
Sonstige Straße: mit Belag / ohne Belag oder in schlechtem Zustand	Other roads: Surfaced / unsurfaced or of doubtful quality
Gesperrte Straße - Im Bau befindliche Straße	Prohibited road - Road under construction
Straßenbreite: getrennte Fahrbahnen / 4, 3 Fahrspuren / 2 breite Fahrspuren / 2 Fahrspuren - 1 Fahrspur / sehr schmale Fahrspur / Wirtschaftsweg / Fußweg	Road width: Dual carriageway / 4 lanes - 3 lanes / 2 wide lanes / 2 lanes - 1 lane / Very narrow road / Cart track / Footpath
Steigungen-Gefälle (Steigung in Pfeilrichtung)	Steepness - Ascent - Descent (ascent in the direction of the arrow)
Paß mit Höhenangabe	Pass and its height above sea level
Schwierige oder gefährliche Strecke	Difficult or dangerous stretch of road
Entfernungen auf der Autobahn: gebührenfreier Abschnitt / gebührenpflichtiger Abschnitt	Distances on motorways: free section / toll section
auf der Straße: Teilentfernung / Gesamtentfernung	on other roads: intermediary / total
Straßennummern	Road classification
Europastraße - Autobahn	International roads - Motorways
Sonstige Straßen	Other roads
Verkehrshindernisse	Obstacles
Zulässige Gesamthöhe (angegeben bis 4 m)	Headroom (given when less than 4 m)
Autofähre	Car ferry
Fußgänger- (und Radfahrer) Fähre	Pedestrian and cycle ferry
Höchstbelastung einer Brücke, einer Fähre (angegeben bis 16 t)	Load limit of a bridge, of a car ferry (given when less than 16t)
Zugbrücke, bewegliche Brücke oder Drehbrücke	Drawbridge or swingbridge
Gesamtgewichtsbeschränkung	Load limit of a road
Einbahnstraße	One way road
Voraussichtliches Datum der Verkehrsfreigabe einer Brücke, einer Straße, etc.	Scheduled opening date of: a bridge, a road, etc.
Bahnlinien	Railways
Haupt- oder Nebenstrecke - Bahnhof	Normal gauge track- Station
Industriegleis oder Straßenbahn	Industrial track or tramway
Zahnradbahn oder Standseilbahn	Rack railway or funicular
Bahnübergänge: schienengleich, Überführung, Unterführung	Level-crossing, railway passing under road, over road
Seilbahn oder Sessellift	Cable-car, chair-lift
Materialtransportbahn	Industrial cable-way

Ortschaften - Verwaltung	Towns - Administration
Rot unterstrichene Orte sind in den Michelin-Führern "Hotels und Restaurants" aufgeführt	The towns or places underlined in red are mentioned in the Michelin red Guides "Hotels and Restaurants"
Stadtplan des Ortes in den selben Führern	Towns having a plan in the Michelin red Guides
Höhenangabe des Ortes	Height above sea level
Provinzgrenze	Provincial boundary
Staatsgrenze - Zollamt	National boundary - Customs post

Theux   (80) Binche

Symbole	Conventional signs
Sehenswürdigkeiten	Sights of interest
Orientierungstafel, Rundblick	Viewing table, panoramic view
Landschaftlich schöne Strecke	Picturesque stretch of road
Aussichtspunkt - Schloß (Burg)	View point - Castle
Kirche oder Kapelle	Church or chapel
Ruine	Ruins
Sonstige Sehenswürdigkeit	Other places of interest
Andere Zeichen	Landmarks
Abgelegenes Hotel oder Restaurant - Festung	Secluded hotel or restaurant - Fort
Kirche - Kapelle - Friedhof	Church - Chapel - Cemetery
Schloß - Ruine - Wegekreuz	Castle - Ruins - Wayside cross
Steinbruch - Bergwerk - Wasserturm	Quarry - Mine - Water tower
Radiosender - Fabrik - Leuchtturm	Radio station - Factory - Lighthouse
Krankenhaus	Hospital
Erdölquelle - Windmühle	Oil well - Windmill
Forsthaus - Talsperre	Forester's lodge - Dam
Forst, Wald	Forest, wood
Staatsforst	State forest
Sport-Fliegerei	Sports-Flying
Golfplatz - Stadion - Pferderennbahn	Golf course - Stadium - Race course
Strand- oder Flußbad - Schwimmbad	Beach or bathing place - Swimming pool
Segelflugplatz	Gliding airfield
Flughafen - Flugplatz	Airport - Airfield

Not much beats the Michelin 1:200,000 map for packing in detail. The sheer range of symbols is breathtaking – not as clear as the Ordnance Survey, but far more varied. (This and other extracts by permission of Michelin, 95-049.)

*Michelin covers far more than simply France. This is the
1:200,000 for the Belgian-Dutch border, with roads marked
from motorways (the E3) to main roads down to tiny lanes.*

43

the Barts Great Britain Road Map series – four for Britain plus two for Ireland – are four miles to an inch. They show all the main roads and many of the lanes, although not always clearly enough to use on a ride.

For novelty I once went away *without* a map, to see where I got to, taking lanes and paths at random. I once also packed a 1930s map of Kent, found in a jumble sale, and kept getting surprised by by-passes, motorways and the absence of railways which the map insisted were there. Great fun, but not the same as a good map.

Maps also wear out. The ink doesn't run, but the paper doesn't stand rain and continual tugging and folding. The Ordnance Survey thought it had solved the problem a few years ago and advertised its coating for a map of the New Forest by submerging one at an exhibition in a glass bowl of goldfish. The map fared well but the Survey admitted later that production problems prevented its going on sale.

The answer is to carry your map on the handlebars. You might have a handlebar bag that holds a map (although most are made for Michelin maps, which fold narrower). The alloy Plescher map carrier

Carry a map on the handlebars for convenience's sake – but take great care about reading it on the move. The protective cover for the map has been removed for the sake of clarity.

Good plastic map clips are available from the CTC shop. The map has been angled only to show the clip better.

bolted to the handlebar stem, and its sprung clamps were of spectac-ular power – enough to carry a pair of gloves, let alone a map. They fell out of fashion along with bolts on handlebar stems, and their plastic replacement is superior. It clips to the handlebars and the exten-sion, and the sheet of plastic folds back to clamp the map. A lot of bike shops don't have them, but they're available from the shop at CTC headquarters.

> **Rule 8** *Put your map in a transparent bag before you push it into the map carrier.*

If you don't it will fall to bits. And, if you don't mind desecrating the covers, the maps fold better if you trim them to the size of the folded map. And while you can read a map on the move, it takes extreme care. So does swooping down hills, because your horizontal map now takes on the function of an aircraft wing and threatens to fly away in the breeze.

Ascents and Descents

But to get back to contours. Nothing's more demoralizing than a road which rolls up and down, up and down, so that the height you gain is immediately lost. Close contours across your road are bad news. Contours running *with* it are good, except that there could be (as there often are alongside rivers) rises and falls steep enough to annoy but never enough to create another contour. It's better to ride with the grain of the land than across it. But if you don't have the choice, ride *up* steep climbs and *down* shallow descents. This might seem odd, but it's true. Steep climbs are short and you can get into bottom gear knowing they'll soon end. You then have a longer, easier ride on the other side. Long drags, on the other hand, are dispiriting, and the steep descent is never relaxing. So you feel cheated.

In the old days the CTC put up 'steep hill' signs – for descents. These days we're more concerned about the ascent. Bad news is a >, or worse, >>. A single > means between 1-in-7 and 1-in-5, or 14 and 20 per cent. The arrows point downhill, so watch out if the injuns are firing in your direction. When they fire double arrows, >>, the hill has tightened to worse than one-in-five. I've ridden one of these on Hard Knott Pass in the Lake District and the effect, once you distinguish it from agony, is that you might tip over backwards. The gradient, says the sign at the bottom with modesty, is 'greater than one-in-three'. It warns:

ROAD UNSUITABLE IN WINTER CONDITIONS
Extreme Caution
Hard Knott Pass
Narrow route Severe bend Gradients Max 30 per cent (1 in 3)
SINGLE TRACK ROAD – use passing places to permit overtaking.

There are three >>s in 450 yards. I don't know why I'm going on about them really – I suppose I was just grateful that I got up (after a fashion). Chevrons are shown only on coloured roads, so there might have been worse.

Allow me to encourage caution. The *Art and Pastime of Cycling*, my favourite cycling book, refers to penny-farthing riders, but it will flash through your thoughts when you make your first out-of-control descent . . .

'A day may come when your machine seems to get beyond your

control, and fairly run away with you. In such a case, if you see that the hill is not very steep, and the bottom is in view . . . then stick to your saddle, keep cool and steer a straight course. . . .

'If, however, you wait too long [to dismount] and the machine is running at, say, 16 or 18 miles an hour, and going quicker each moment . . . you must not, no matter what the cost, stick to the saddle. . . .

'If you find you are unable to dismount owing to the pace and steepness of the gradient, go for the nearest hedge or hawthorn bush and, just as you approach, throw your legs over the handles. You are sure to be hurt, but you may escape with only a few scrapes and bruises, whereas to hold on means more or less injury. If no hedge or hawthorn bush is near, throw your legs over the handles and put the brake hard on, and you will shoot forward and alight on your feet, when you must make every effort to keep on your feet and run as hard as you can, for your bicycle is in eager pursuit, and a stroke from it may place you *hors de combat*.'

Riding down a hill without terror is the same as taking a corner quickly. Assuming you can see far enough to brake safely and be sure no red-faced man with a flat cap and a chequered shirt is about to drive a tractor from a hedge, you can swoosh through bends like Franz Klammer. All you have to do is watch the *inside* of the bends . . . and, to repeat, to be sure you're safe.

A car cornered too fast rolls away from the corner. The same would happen on a bike but it's impossible to corner without leaning inwards. You don't steer a bike, you lean in so far beyond its centre of gravity that it threatens to fall over; then you turn the front wheel to prop it up. While the wheels keep moving, the prop stays in line and you balance. If the tyre slips or you get the angle wrong, you break the triangle of the bike, wheel and corner and you fall over, although into the bend and not out of it. The easiest way to break the triangle is to look *outside* the bend. So . . .

- Look down at a point a yard ahead and inside your front wheel.
- Straighten the leg on the outside of the bike and place most of your weight on it.
- Shift your weight to the outside arm and lower your centre of gravity, if you have dropped handlebars, by holding the bottom of the bars.
- Point your bent knee towards your route out of the corner.

Do all this and you'll get down as fast as the grip of your tyres allows. Want another rule? OK.

> **Rule 9** *Always ride a hill slowly and evenly.*

Speed rather than distance kills. Push hard, and your internal meter goes into the red and you'll repay the cost for the rest of the day. The energy for a 1-in-27, just a drag, increases wildly with speed. Purists

MPH	6	10	15	20	22	24
Rolling resistance	6	10	15	20	22	24
Wind resistance	2	9	31	74	99	128
Energy for hill	**40**	**67**	**100**	**133**	**147**	**160**

(*International Cycling Guide*, 1980)

said to stay in the saddle and change down gear until you'd mastered even the toughest climb. They relied on deft movements called ankling to claw the pedal round at the bottom before pulling it back up with the toe strap. Well, I can't get up a steep hill on just that and I don't know anybody who can. I suspect ankling died out with men in deer-stalker hats and long socks.

Pick a gear you can turn a little less slowly than on the level. If you under-gear – some people get their knees going like bluebottle wings – you will burn more energy, decelerate disturbingly fast and make dispiriting progress. Place your hands on the brake hoods or the flat centre of the bars (or its equivalent on mountain-bike or sports bars), bend your elbows and move back to stretch your legs. Drop into an even rhythm, smooth rather than stabbing. Pull on the pedals if you have toe straps or clip-on shoes.

Get out the saddle for the toughest bits, or to gain momentum, then return. You can take a hill faster out of the saddle – the French call it *en danseuse* and we say honking – but at greater expense. Change gear as the road flattens; it hardly seems to matter up or down as long as your legs and lungs get a break. When the climb toughens again, go back into climbing position. You can have gears so low that your pedals turn faster than the wheels. But if you go too low – and anything approaching one-to-one is too low – it's hard to control the bike and it's possible to lift the front wheel if the back's loaded.

In a car you're concerned only whether you're in first, second or third and so on. The proportions bother nobody but the engineer. On a bike, they're important. The bike-engine is flexible on the flat, but bikes are inefficient against gravity. Small changes in gear become important. The ratio between pedal and wheel speed is given a number. A 52-inch gear has the rolling distance of 52-inch diameter wheel.

Nobody thinks of penny-farthings when they talk of gear sizes, nobody worries *exactly* what the equivalent dimension would be, and nobody does the calculation himself (teeth on chainwheel × wheel size in inches ÷ teeth on rear sprocket) because it's easier to consult a gear table. On the Continent they quote gears by how far one turn of the pedals takes you. The calculation is wheel circumference × teeth on chainring ÷ teeth on sprocket.

Experienced riders use derailleur gears, which switch the chain from one rear sprocket or one chainring to another by pulling a lever. They were temperamental in novice hands, but index-gearing (notches which get the right gear) have removed most of the dangers. Hub gears are more reliable and last for decades. A derailleur wears out both itself and chains, and clogs with mud. The trouble with hub gears such

Good quality chainsets have changeable rings; the tiniest give you a gear range to get you and your camping gear over the Alps.

49

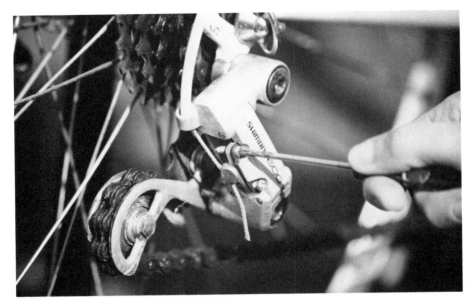

How far outward the derailleur swings – and whether it jumps off the smallest sprocket – is controlled by adjusting the higher screw, which presses against a backplate to prevent further movement . . .

. . . and the bottom gear, therefore, is adjusted with the lower screw.

Extra-low gears use more chain. Fit a derailleur with a longer
than usual jockey arm to compensate.

as the legendary Sturmey-Archer is that the gap between gears is
selected by the factory. You can shift the whole lot up or down by
changing the sprocket or the chainring, but the relationship of top to
middle to bottom is unchanged. A derailleur gives up to 21 gears (not
all usable, admittedly) but most hub gears have only three. Sadly, you
can't take out a hub-gear wheel and switch to derailleurs. Hub gears
are narrower and the frame is therefore also narrower. You're committed unless you can afford a new frame and wheels. By that time you
might as well consider a new bike.

Look for gears spaced evenly from 40 to 90 for everyday riding and
down to 32 for loaded touring. Even 32 should be treated with caution,
and anything higher than 90 is for belting down hills or when there's
a gale at your back.

5

Bunches of Roadies

Cycling's hospitable. You can chase around on a long lone race through hell, but what's the point? The riding's a pleasure, the rhythmic relaxation and bouts of exercise, but the ability to stop, stare and chat is a bonus. Most people want to ask where you're going. The world in general and pubs in particular are full of people who *used* to be cyclists. They can't think why they no longer are, but that's not important. I once got talking to a chap in Cheshire who insisted on fetching his friend's wife. I ate my pie-and-two-veg, wondering who and why, and eventually he returned with a shrivelled lady with bright eyes and a speed of walking that belied her stoop.

In a voice with a trace of the original French, she said she had been in the Resistance during the war (a not unusual claim) and an acquaintance of a man called Georges Speicher. The name meant little until she said he'd been world cycling champion in 1933 after being hauled out of a nightclub at three that morning and taken to the circuit at Montlhéry. The French hadn't selected him because he'd won the Tour de France and they thought he'd be too tired. Then they changed their mind and scoured Pigalle to find him. 'He was always known to us as Gorgeous Georges,' the little old lady said. Wonderful.

Riding with other people is also easier. When the going gets hard you share the lead. Half the energy at 10mph is to push aside the air and the rest is to overcome rolling resistance. Ambling is therefore easy. Gareth Lovett Jones, in his celebration of slow cycling called *English Country Lanes*, calls it 'pootling', combining pedal and footle, of which he says: 'The pootlist is never shamefaced or apologetic – indeed he is quite the opposite – in discussing the fact that he has done nothing very much and, what is more, has done it randomly, and taken rather a lot of time over it.'

On the other hand, 13mph will get you to the café before it shuts, and 22mph will zip you along with energy you never thought you had. Hol Crane, of the astonishing family Crane (Nick and Dick rode into central China to find the centre of the earth – land furthest from the sea in all directions – and up and down Mount Kilimanjaro), says the change from rolling to wind resistance is so great that at the racing speed of 30mph all but 10 per cent of the effort is for the air alone. It's because rolling resistance rises in proportion to the speed, whereas wind resistance is the *cube* of the speed.

MPH	6	10	15	20	22	24	26	28	30	32
Rolling	6	10	15	20	22	24	26	28	30	32
Air	2	9	31	74	99	128	163	203	250	303

(International Cycling Guide, 1980)

Therefore the faster you ride, the more it helps to be behind someone. Another cyclist is as bulky as you are and cuts through the air provided you stay a foot from his back wheel. Entire trains are more effective: Mile-a-Minute Murphy clocked 60mph behind a train in 1898 and wiped the smile off those who laughed when he said he could follow anything provided he was sheltered. Racing cyclists have this technique perfected. The author Fred DeLong says a feature of 1930s training rides was the chuffing of riders' tyres on the wheel in front.

If you maintain your speed into a headwind, your air speed rises and, with it, your energy. Experienced cyclists share the lead. One rides in front for half a mile, the other sheltering, and then they change. Groups, such as a CTC club ride, ride line-astern in pairs, the front pair dropping back after 5 or 10 miles and everyone moving up. Only the leader, who's got to choose the way, stays in front all day (which is why he is the first to stare out of his window for trees bent horizontal by wind).

Rule 10 *Everybody has to watch where he's going, but those in front have a better view.*

So, if you see a pothole, horse dung, or you're stopping or slowing, shout the message. If you don't, you'll count the cost in grazed knees, broken mudguards, bent wheels and bad humour.

The way to work out the speed is with distance and available time (remember those physics lessons?). Spread your finger and thumb against the scale on the map. If you're lucky, it'll match some useful distance. My span is 18cm which with a few wiggles in the lane is ten kilometres on a Landranger, or about five miles without the wiggles.

You then have to guess how fast you'll ride. Once you know how far you rode in an hour the first time you tried – and car milometers are accurate – you extend the calculation. But remember that an hour's ride provides few distractions and only a little tiredness, whereas on longer distances you'll stop, look around and eat, and you'll get weary. Always underestimate your speed. You can paddle in a stream or drink tea if you're early; it's rarely fun riding hard to get back before dark.

CTC Sections

The modern CTC badge has the old winged-wheel symbol set within it. The CTC of the old badge was originally in gothic type.

Distances go faster in company, and headwinds diminish. But social riding is a thing of the past in many clubs, which is a shame. Members get together only to train for races, and sometimes not even for that. Luckily, it continues unabated in the clubs, or sections, of the CTC. Most members ride individually, or at least not in organized groups, but there are nevertheless 200 sections for social riding, club evenings and other events. All welcome new members, however inexperienced. Many have rides for casual riders, with quaint titles such as easyriders, but ask about the distance because some are for fitter members (hardriders, to distinguish them) and might be 90 miles. Most days won't go much beyond 40 miles. If that still sounds a long way, remember Alan Leng's comment that 8mph covers 40 miles in five hours, giving you the rest of the day. The speed is likely to be 12–14mph, harder than 8mph but not as much as you'd think. Even beginners exceed 10mph. And don't worry about being left behind – the pace is the speed of the slowest rider, and there'll be others walking hills alongside you. But do ask, because you'll want to know you're physically and mechanically self-dependent.

Sections print lists of weekend rides, often duplicated in monthly magazines full of stories, nick-names and in-jokes. They name stops for mid-morning drinks and lunch and, less usually, an afternoon stop. All-day rides are giving way to home-after-lunch. And oh yes . . .

CTC signs are rare these days. Once they were on hotels and cafés recommended by members . . .

. . . now they survive on quite unlikely premises. This one, in its original black and white, is in Fakenham, Norfolk.

> **Rule 11** *Always ask, regardless of what it says on the sheet, what time the ride will actually start.*

Cyclists have anarchic views of time and the fact that you've turned up ten minutes late and found no one there could mean either that they've left or that everybody's yet to turn up.

Sections group into sixty district associations. They run all the national events, including the Birthday Rides – thousands of cyclists meeting since 1970 in the week of 5 August to mark the CTC's founding. The CTC also has a racing competition over 25, 50 and 100 miles for men; 10, 25 and 50 for women. The prize is presented at the CTC dinner, held in a different venue each winter.

By far the most valuable benefits of membership are the third party insurance, free legal aid and the touring service. CTC lawyers have secured up to a quarter of a million pounds for members. If the accident is *your* fault, the CTC will represent you and use its free third-party insurance to pay the bill (up to a limit, but it's enormous). There was a time, says CTC director Alan Harlow, that folk regarded cyclists as paupers and not worth suing. But no more. 'The public,' he says, 'now realize that the rider of an expensive bike has got money!' The touring department has the experience of the millions who've been members over the years. I'm sure there's never a question that's had it stumped. Its drawers are stuffed with leaflets, pamphlets, cross-referenced advice cards and several hundred place-to-place and circular rides all over Britain. The technical department has a mastery of boffinry which I find breathtaking. Just ask. It's all free.

Join by writing to the CTC at Godalming – a phone call will give you the current rates and your nearest officials – or by calling at Cotterell House, 69 Meadrow, Godalming, Surrey GU7 3HS. Meadrow is the main road on the Guildford side of Godalming, the A3100, and CTC headquarters are in a detached building set back from the north side between King's Road and Hare Lane. It's a short ride from Farncombe station on the Waterloo–Portsmouth line. The shop has one of the country's biggest stocks of cyclists' maps. It's open Monday to Friday from 8.30am to 5pm and, mysteriously, 'on some Saturdays'.

Membership brings you six issues a year of *Cycle Touring & Campaigning* (unkindly known for its occasional glum state-of-the-nation reports as *Cycle Touring & Complaining*), competitive rates for theft insurance, and so much cycling advice that you could spend more time reading about it than carrying it out!

£1.95 (free to members)

CT&C

CYCLE TOURING AND CAMPAIGNING

The Cyclists' Touring Club's magazine

February/March 1995

Easter in Turkey · Tipperary quickie
Two portable bikes reviewed

Cycle Touring & Campaigning – *it was described once as
'strangely fabulous, as if another Britain existed filled with
country lanes, thatched cottages, fields and rolling hills . . . the
modern world is mentioned from time to time, in the full
knowledge of every reader's disapproval.'*

Touring in Ireland

CTC Local Touring Adviser, Billy McCormick, Co Down, writes: 'With the ceasefire and return to normality, hopefully tourists will again be visiting Northern Ireland in large numbers and indeed a big increase in visitors is expected this year. I can assure you that they will

all receive a very warm welcome.'

Billy notes that a large new youth hostel has recently opened near the centre of Belfast (Donegall Pass) and adds that Northern Ireland is a great place for a cycling holiday.

Belfast member Paddy McAteer has written to point out that in addition to the sheets of the 1:50

000 map series covering the whole of Ireland listed on the CTC Shop pages in the December/January issues, the 18 sheets which cover Northern Ireland have all been issued. If not available from the CTC Shop, they may be obtained from the Ordnance Survey of Northewrn Ireland, Colby House, Stranmillis Court, Belfast BT9 5BJ. He also points out that for the long-distance Irish tourer, the four sheets of the OS Holiday 1:250 000 series which cover the whole of the island would be more practical. These are up to date – which is certainly not true of the remaining one-inch and half-inch sheets.

Information about touring in the whole island of Ireland is available free of charge from CTC Touring Department. The Ireland Touring Information Booklet includes advice on which sheets of the 1:50 000 series are currently available, updated as new sheets are published. Also available is an up-to-date listing of Local Touring Advisers who can offer further advice. Please send in an A5 sized SAE with your membership number.

obtain from the Touring Department is available to CTC members who send an SAE marked 'Touring list' to CTC Touring Department. Please quote your membership number.

Rural camping in Brittany

Helen and John Edge have opened a small campsite about 3km from the medieval Breton town of Josselin, and they specially welcome cycling visitors. The site, which at present has only 8 pitches, is also only about 1km north of the River Oust towpath, which runs from Nantes to Brest. Breakfast is available, and caravan hire is possible. Details: Camping des Cerisiers, Brancillet, 56800 Guillac, Morbihan, France; tel (from UK) 00 33 97 75 61 24.

Countryside Commission and English Nature not to merge

It seems that the threatened shotgun merger of the Countryside Commission and English Nature has been called off – at least for the present. An announcement by Environment Secretary, John Gunmmer, in October confirmed that a programme of closer working between the two bodies rather than a merger is to be developed.

PPG9 for wildlife sites

Planning Policy Guidance Note 9 from the Department of the Environment advises on the planning

implications of regulations which implement the EC Habitats Directive. These came into force on 30 October. An important feature of the regulations is that they prevent the granting of permitted development rights under the General Development Order which would adversely affect any area designated under the Birds or Wildlife Directive. PPG9 (ISBN 0 11 752787 4) is available from HMSO, price £8.50.

Bicycle Beanos again

Bicycle Beano, who have made their name in cycling holidays with wholefood vegetarian cuisine are celebrating their 14th season this year. For 1995 there are eight week-long holidays in Wales and

the Welsh border counties – with accommodation ranging from a priory on the Pembrokeshire coast to camping in the middle Wye valley. Distances range from 30 to 60 miles per day, and prices are from £240 per person. Details: Bicycle Beano, Erwood, Builth Wells, Powys LD2 3PQ; (01982) 560471.

The dirt on Rhayader

Clive and his mum are still at it: ski-instructor turned mountainbiker Clive Powell is running his Dirty Weekends and other mountain-bike happenings again for 1995. The weekends include leading and tuition over the numerous tracks of the Elan Valley (Clive is a qualified coach), while accommodation and – most important – food are in the hands of Clive's mother Pam. Never-ending pots of tea and home-made cakes when you come in tired and muddy are a definite promise. Bikes can be brought, bought or hired. Details and dates (weekends start 28 April): Clive Powell Mountain-Bikes, The Mount, East Street, Rhayader, Powys LD6 5DN; tel (01597) 810585/811343; fax (01597) 810585.

General news

New public cycle show – Bike '95

Although the trade has its own excellent show in Harrogate, hosted by the Bicycle Association, of recent years there has been a dearth of bike shows open to the public, with Cyclex folding in 1993 and Ibex 1994 being still-born. Now, *writes Lisa Warburton*, Future Events has stepped into the breach with Bike '95. This new exhibition is to be held at Olympia, London, from 7-9 April – probably the best time of year from the cyclist's point of view.

All days are open to the general public, and an array of activities accompany the main exhibition. They include a Trials Area for you to learn and improve your skills and stunts, a specially designed indoor MTB track for you to test the latest technology and a Bike Build Up section where you can find out the latest tricks of the trade from builders at the show.

The Hub will be the place to find experts or the occasional celebrity or you can pit yourself against a racing cyclist or friend in the Fitness Area. The Great Outdoors will be allocated to touring and commuting, and there is also space set

aside to Concept Bikes, Recumbent Racing and a BMX Freestyle Display.

Come along to the CTC's stand (near the Outdoor Feature) and have a chat. We will be there to meet members and answer your queries, and persuade other cyclists to join us.

Cycling adventurer and Honorary CTC Member Nick Crane will be presenting a lecture on cycling. He will also be on the CTC's stand to answer questions or sign books – don't miss him! Also with us will be the recently-formed CTC Off-Road and of course the CTC Shop.

We've negotiated a discount of 10% off the entrance fee for CTC members – but only if you quote your CTC membership number. There are more details on the back cover of this issue.

Bike '95 seems to be a serious attempt to provide us with a national cycle exhibition encompassing the many aspects of cycling. Let's hope that the industry takes note and supports a much-needed public show.

GDBA seeks pilots

The Guide Dogs for the Blind Association organises activity holi-

days for visually-impaired people, including – for 1995 – tandem holidays. These range from introductory days to a week's tour in France. However, they are short of sighted front riders (who receive a reduced-price holiday in recognition of their contribution). If you are interested, please contact: Ian Jones, GDBA Adventure Group, Unit 9, Dockray Hall Industrial Estate, Kendal, Cumbria LA9 4RU; (01539) 735080.

1995 Tandem Club rallies

The Tandem Club is organising three rallies this year. The first is an International Rally at Carnac in Brittany from 27 May to 3 June. The second, organised in association with Cykelframjandet of Sweden, is at Helsingborg from 30 July to 5 August. Back home, the Tandem Club's own National Rally will be held in Kent from 18 to 21 August. Camping and other accommodation will be available at all three events. Details are available from: David and Carolyn McHale, 3 Eriboll Close, Linslade, Leighton Buzzard, Beds LU7 7XW; (01525) 381505.

. . . And the reality: pages of detailed information on riding a bike, technical problems answered, and news of safety campaigns . . . plus a little, elsewhere, of that 'strangely fabulous' world.

6

A Bed for the Night

There was once a chap in Essex called Walter Stolle. He was odd, even his friends say that, but he was an adventurer. He never knew when to stop. Most of us go out for the day, enjoy ourselves and come back. We might sometimes go for a weekend, perhaps even a fortnight. But Walter waved goodbye in January 1959 and I'm not sure he ever came back. I remember reading that in just 1974 he'd ridden 22,060 miles, through Nigeria, Niger, Dahomey, Togo, Upper Volta, Ghana, Ivory Coast, Liberia, Sierra Leone, Liberia and Guinea. All these are some way from Essex and Walter had spent the previous years getting there by tortuous routes of his own.

He made his living with slide shows in seven languages. He'd given 2,500 in fifteen years and had his bike stolen half a dozen times. And then I met Ian Hibell, a man as rowdy as a dormouse, who wears shorts even in snow and lives with his mother Dot in a 400-year-old cottage above Brixham in Devon. And yet this gentle man who worried he might work for Standard Telephones for the rest of his life could think of only three countries he hadn't cycled in, had ridden a quarter of a million miles from the North Cape of Norway to the Cape of Good Hope in South Africa, from Tierra del Fuego across the Andes to Alaska, and come face-to-face with tsetse flies, cross men with spears, charging elephants, and more. People told him he'd be unwise to cycle the Sahara, especially with a fever. And after a while he wondered whether they might be right.

'Every step,' he told me, 'became a very great ordeal. It would require all your strength, with no reserve left over. You'd set your sights on the next kilometre post, if you could see it, and when you got there the only shade you would get would be standing against the post – this thin band of shade. It was quite agonizing and I couldn't really see how I could possibly make it.'

He abandoned his bike in a delirium of thirst and exhaustion to stop camel caravans for water. Normally they or desert trucks would pass every eighteen hours. This time they failed to appear for three days and he ran out.

'I thought I couldn't survive by day, so I'd navigate by night, by the stars, and in the morning I'd find the first marker post and get back to the main track and sit it out until I either perish or they find me. But I didn't find it.'

He left his bike in the sand, along with his last two pints of water, to make searching easier. But he could find neither his bike nor foot tracks through the bushes.

'Now I stood there with nothing at all. As the day wore on, it started to get really hot. My tongue started to fur over and my whole mouth was dry and I couldn't swallow. And now I didn't bother to look for the bicycle – I was looking for somewhere comfortable to die.

'I knew that this was surely the end. I stood there wondering how much longer I'd have to put up with it, and at what point you start to go mad, and I turned around and there in all the heat haze was the most Biblical-looking apparition. A figure seemed to be waving, coming closer to me. I identified it as a very small donkey, with a figure on it. I thought maybe I really had passed on and gone to better places. But it was real, and there were two little kids sitting on the back of a donkey, towing a tiny white camel.

'I couldn't even croak. And they had no water to offer me.' He drew a bicycle in the sand and gestured rewards for finding it. They took him there within ten minutes. Nothing had been touched. Hibell swallowed the water and wondered about the reward.

'The only thing I had was a bag of sweets to help me get through the desert, and it was torn from my grasp. By now other little children had arrived. At this point a real Tuareg turned up, in the dark head-dress and the long robe and a great big sword at his waist, and also a stick. And he waded in and started to beat the kids, and then *he* wanted a reward.

'Now, this was very, very difficult for me because at one stage I was willing to give everything I owned just to live. But just as soon as I recovered my equipment, I wasn't so sure. But I had a tube of nose ointment, and I presented it to him and tried to indicate its use, and he didn't look at all pleased, of course, because he hardly needed any sun-tan ointment on his particular nose. But he took it, very reluctantly, and I was really passing out with a grey mist across my eyes. I knew that I was losing my senses. The next thing I was aware of was my head being thrust between my knees and ice-cold water being thrown over me. It saved my life.'

I tell you this because Hibell's obsession started when his father Les couldn't afford the fare for the whole family to Hove. Hibell's mother and brother went by train and the two older men cycled, at least once sleeping on a bench. Perhaps you should be warned that an afternoon's ride to a bed-and-breakfast in the next county could be the start of a slippery slope. People get carried away because, as Gareth Lovett Jones put it in *English Country Lanes*:

'The urban Englishman retains some mental image of a better world "out there" beyond the most recent extensions of the urban fringe, where the motorway does not (yet) penetrate. . . . He holds on to this image self-amusedly, perhaps even self-critically. Yet despite all the disclaimers he may make, it persists for him as something *almost* real. In this abstractly ideal rural world . . . some form of better life may perhaps, somehow, be lived, if not necessarily by him . . .

'Some country people are just as prone to it. A lady who sold me two ambrosial doughnuts in a cake shop in Sturminster Newton, Dorset . . . told me with delight and a contagious sense of magic how she was going to drive down to Devon with her children. . . . It was as if, somehow, rural Devon was more special than rural mid-Dorset: *Devon*, for her, was the great Beyond.'

Staying away for the night adds adventure to enjoyment. You can be the most jaded stay-away salesman in the world, but pitching up somewhere in late afternoon on a bike is an experience you'd never guess. Apart from the happiness of somewhere new, of an enjoyable day, of finding a place to eat and wander in a summer evening, there's the fuss. It's as though they've never had a cyclist before (perhaps they haven't). Copious tea will be pressed on you 'because you've ridden so far,' and you'll be cosseted and fretted over. I kept in touch for years with a family near Letterkenny for whose star-struck daughter I cadged a ticket for *Top of the Pops* (which is also shown in Ireland). She was delighted. I imagine that prayers are still said to me nightly.

I suppose there are hotels where relaxing cyclists clink glasses and beckon the barman through potted palms, but I don't know them and I don't think I'd like the cyclists either. I don't expect to doss because I'm a cyclist, but I ride a bike to stay in touch with the world, not divorce myself from it nightly.

Bed and Breakfasts

B-and-Bs are cheaper and frequently more comfortable than even medium-grade hotels. There are more of them, the owners are friend-lier, the drive for better facilities means many aren't far short of luxurious . . . and there's all that tea.

'Twasn't always that way, though. The *Daily News* had a cycling correspondent called Kuklos – Fitzwater Wray – who got very uppity about things like gear cases (gadgets to protect you from the chain and vice versa), which he dismissed as 'laced-up things of bad leather and celluloid . . . worse than useless', and frauds in which poorly made bikes were passed off as private bargains – 'Officer going to Mesopotamia must sell much-loved mount', etc. He also reckoned that one shirt 'is good for a week, even when worn day and night'.

Anyway, Kuklos's advice on choosing accommodation was to demand to see the room and then to push a mirror between the sheets. If it re-emerged misted, the bed was damp. But whether it was damp or dry, no one should be charged more than six shillings for bed and breakfast. Five was a fairer price, but anything cheaper than that and there'd be a good chance of finding someone in bed with you in the morning.

There are more B-and-Bs every year as people with a spare bedroom raise a few pounds for no great expense. Most are in touring areas – it's impossible to be more than 150 yards from a B-and-B or a cream-tea café in Devon or Cornwall – but there's a healthy sprinkling everywhere. Most people know the bed-and-breakfast area in their town – usually large houses split into flats and hotels – so always ask. If you don't like finding one as you ride, contact the tourist informa-tion office. They're marked on the OS map with a blue *i*, and you've probably got one, however small, near home. Libraries and town halls have areas set aside – piles of leaflets and Holiday in Britain booklets and well-meaning assistants with glasses and cardigans. Some offices book a bed while you wait, at little or no charge, which can save hours of wandering in such areas as York and Chester. And most can give you a thin booklet of all the tourist offices in the country, which can be more useful than you'd imagine.

National Tourist Boards

The national tourist boards in the UK are:

British Travel Centre (personal callers only), 12 Regent Street, Piccadilly Circus, London SW1Y 4PQ.

Northern Ireland, River House, 48 High Street, Belfast BT1 2DS (tel.: 01232-231221; fax: 01232-240960).
Scotland, 23 Ravelston Terrace, Edinburgh EH4 3EU (tel.: 0131-332 2433).
Wales, Brunel House, 2 Fitzalan Road, Cardiff CF2 1UY (tel.: 01222-499909; fax: 01222-485031).
Jersey, Weighbridge, St Helier, Jersey (tel.: 01534-78000; fax: 01534-35569).
Guernsey, PO Box 23, White Rock, Guernsey (tel.: 01481-26611; fax: 01481-21246).
Isle of Man, Sea Terminal Building, Douglas (tel.: 01624-74323; fax: 01624-72872).

Regional Tourist Offices

Regional centres have more local information and save the trouble of phoning several counties.

Cumbria, Ashleigh, Holly Road, Windermere LA23 2AQ (tel.: 019662-4444; fax: 019662-4041).
East Anglia, Topplesfield Hall, Hadleigh IP7 5DN (tel.: 01473-822922; fax: 01473-823063).
Heart of England, Woodside, Larkhill, Worcester WR5 2EF (tel.: 01905-763436; fax: 01905-763450).
London, 26 Grosvenor Gardens, London SW1W 0DU (tel.: 0171-730 3450; fax: 0171-730 9367).
North-West, The Last Drop Village, Bromley Cross, Bolton BL7 9PZ (tel.: 01204-591511; fax: 01204-595238).
Northumbria, Aykley Heads, Durham DH1 5UX (tel.: 0191-384 6905; fax: 0191-386 0899).
South-East, The Old Brew House, Warwick Park, Tunbridge Wells TN2 5TA (tel.: 01892-540766; fax: 01892-511088).
South, 40 Chamberlayne Road, Eastleigh SO5 5JH (tel.: 01703-620006; fax: 01703-620010).
Thames and Chilterns, The Mount House, Church Green, Witney OX8 6DZ (tel.: 01993-778800; fax: 01993-779152).
West Country, Trinity Court, 27 Suthernhay East, Exeter EX1 1QS (tel.: 01392-76351; fax: 01392-420891).
Yorkshire and Humberside, 312 Tadcaster Road, York YO2 2HF (tel.: 01904-707961; fax: 01904-701414).

A phone call will bring you a list of B-and-Bs and hotels. You can then phone before you set off or, my usual method, leave it till lunchtime to make your afternoon as long as the weather and your freshness allow. But remember that leaving it late means your first choice may be full.

> **Rule 12** *Find somewhere away from the road; you've already had a hard day and you don't want traffic to keep you awake all night.*

Farmhouses are ideal and I've always had success with *Farm Holidays in Britain* published by the Farm Holiday Bureau. It costs about £3, but 'in Britain' excludes Scotland. Each entry has a sketch of the building, a description and an OS reference (not always dependable). W.H. Smith and the like stock them, but if you can't find one, try the bureau at the National Agricultural Centre, Stoneleigh, near Kenilworth CV8 2LZ.

The CTC has two schemes. In one, members put up tourists who in turn are prepared to put up them or other cyclists in return. The addresses, therefore, are available only to those taking part. Then there's the CTC handbook, which lists hotels and B-and-Bs recommended by members. The list has much improved over recent years, although it was once small and inconsistent – there were clearly members who approved of sleeping next to a main road. Now there's more consistency and a wider choice, and the handbook, bless it, also lists cyclists' cafés, open on Sundays and accustomed to their patrons' eccentricities. Both sections are updated each year.

Youth Hostels

The one thing I ask of a night's stop is a good rest. It's because of noise that I stopped hostelling. Some of my happiest holidays have been to hostels here and abroad, but the rumpus finally got to me. Hostels have become paying propositions and less idealistic, and the barrier against (in theory) all but cyclists and walkers lifted years ago. They compete by booking school parties. And whatever else school parties do during the day, tiring themselves out is not one. I ask only for a good night's sleep. I don't want, as I was after a day across the Irish mountains, to be kept awake until 3am by brawling kids whom their teacher had shrewdly put into one dormitory (mine) while he had gone to sleep in another. I got my revenge by waking him at 1am and then again at 2.30 to demand he restore order, which displeased him

*You want solitude and beautiful surroundings? Head for remote
youth hostels. The mountains of Skye overlook Raasay, and a boat
brings visitors to Ravadennan.*

Or you can have elegant grandeur, of course. This is Perth youth hostel.

but made me feel better, but next day I was so tired that I completed my journey to Dublin by train. I have never stayed at a hostel since.

Peter Knottley wrote in *Cycling* as long ago as 1967: 'I rode 85 miles to Inglesham youth hostel the other day – a slack time of year, midweek, and thus unbooked. This 20-bed hostel had 19 bookings, 17 of which consisted of a single school group. The warden had (I wonder why?) left the booking diary on the reception desk for all to see, and I duly saw and stole away.'

Many cyclists do still tour from hostel to hostel and enjoy themselves. There are times when I think my reluctance to join them is simply middle-aged grumpiness because hostels are still pretty popular with the under-20s. Hostels offer the companionship of other travellers and the chance to meet another cyclist (you rarely meet another cyclist at a B-and-B). You can stay in a Norman castle, manor houses, cheese factories, water mills and stately homes. Tanner Hatch in Surrey is sublime – a cottage deep in a wood, reached by muddy path and equipped with a wood fire and scorched armchairs. All but the most remote are signposted from the road by a symbol of a house

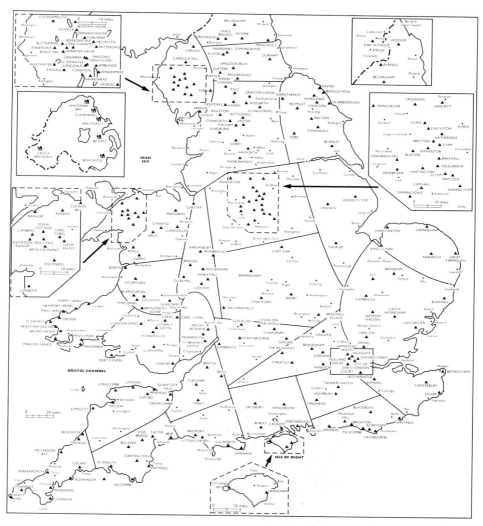

Hostels all over the place – there are so many in England and Wales that you're never more than a comfortable day's ride from the next.

and a tree and then, closer by, by a triangular sign bearing the initials of the appropriate organization.

Hostels belonging to the national groups are shown on the OS map as a red triangle. There are around 400 in Britain and northern and southern Ireland. And the word 'youth' is misleading. Despite the school parties, British and Irish hostels open to all ages, although you'll need an adult with you if you're younger than twelve. You can join at the hostel. Hostel associations publish maps and details. Generally hostels shut by day, because the warden's got work to do. Many also close one day a week and parts of the winter. Check the handbook.

When you arrive, lock your bike in the shed, walk to the entrance and find the warden. Check there's room if you haven't booked. You can book by post or the previous day by phone, but if you haven't there's usually a notice on the door explaining if the hostel still has beds; rural hostels usually have room even in midsummer, but their city-centre cousins in York and London, or in areas such as Stratford-upon-Avon, fill early in the evening.

Go into the hostel, sign the house book, and hand over your membership card. Wardens vary as much as their buildings, from the eccentric to the dour. I once fancied becoming a hostel warden; I gave up when three wardens in a row told me I was mad even to consider the idea. So forgive a warden if you catch him on an off-day.

Evening meals are around 6.30 if they're provided, but it's best to book. Ask when you get to the hostel. Not every hostel warden cooks,

Many youth hostels serve meals. This is Crianlarich. A hint for all hostels – consider cooking your own breakfast, so that you can get away more quickly in the morning.

but there's always a kitchen crammed with strapping Australian girls called Nolene and Charlene and blond Germans wearing shorts and leather sandals, stirring things glumly in pots. You can buy milk by the half pint, individual tea bags, bread by the slice, and almost anything in a tin. It might not be *cordon bleu*, but it's what you make it. You can always shop on the way although, as Peter Knottley discovered, you might have trouble persuading a supermarket to sell you a single egg. His piece in *Cycling* on persuading a supermarket manager that if hens laid eggs one by one there was no reason he should have to buy them by the half dozen was one of his most entertaining. It might seem pedantic, but there's little room (or need) to carry surplus food.

You'll find blankets folded on your bed. The warden will rent you a sheet sleeping-bag, which you hand back in the morning; or you can buy your own once you're a regular hosteller. Wild living's not expected, so the door closes at lights-out.

> **Rule 13** *Cook your own breakfast even if you book an evening meal.*

And if the fashion at the hostel is to do a small job to defray the cost, do it that night. You can then get away by 8.30a.m. while the stair-sweepers and spud-peelers are still busy. Collect your card and admire the stamp on the hostels-visited page. I built a massive collection and moved the loose pages from one card to the next. I'd have been wiser to leave them at home; the whole lot got soaked on an extraordinary day to Ivinghoe, near Luton, and they were never the same.

Never one to learn quickly, I ruined the lot for good four years later when my bike, saddlebag and contents slid off railings and fell into Kinsale harbour in Ireland. A fisherman pulled it out with a grappling hook and two ladies at the only launderette supervised the tumble-dryer. I shall never forget their looks as my cheque book, YHA card and paperback disintegrated amid shirts, underpants and jumpers.

Unwashed membership cards are valid all over the world, but only those issued by the main associations. They are:

YHA for England and Wales, Trevelyan House, 8 St Stephen's Hill, St Albans AL1 2DY (tel.: 01727-55215).
Scottish YHA, 7 Glebe Crescent, Stirling FK8 2JA (tel.: 01786-2821).
YHA of Northern Ireland, 56 Bradbury Place, Belfast BT7 1RU (tel.: 01203-324733).
An Oige, 39 Mountjoy Square, Dublin 1. (tel.: from the UK 00-353-1-363111).

There are unaffiliated, independent hostels and camping barns. They're open, as hostels originally were, to cyclists and walkers. Ask about camping barns at the Peak National Study Centre at Losehill Hall, Castleton S30 2WB; independent hostels are listed from time to time in *CT&C*. The magazine also lists the CTC's own holidays at home and abroad, at fixed centres and moving on. They're run and led by experienced members and the range is enormous. I can highly recommend them. Holidays run by commercial companies, sometimes with luggage carried by van, are also advertised.

Luggage

Here is what I recommend you take for different distances:

A half-day ride

Waterproofs (usually a cape)
Puncture repair kit
3 tyre levers (plastic is now as strong as and lighter than metal)
Spare jumper in spring and autumn
Gloves and hat in winter

A weekend ride, staying in a B-and-B

Everything above, plus:
Washing gear (packed on top so that I can freshen myself up in a loo)
Trousers, shirt, shoes, socks, etc. for the evening
Spare underclothes
Spare rear brake cable (which will also fit the derailleur gear)
Chain rivet extractor
Spoke adjustment key
Small adjustable spanner
Two spare spokes (taped to a mudguard stay)

A weekend ride, staying at youth hostels

Everything above, plus:
Towel (provided at a B-and-B)
Sheet sleeping-bag
YHA membership card and handbook

Several days

Everything above, plus:
Soap powder for shirts and underwear
Tiny hair dryer (useful for drying clothes!)
Spare shirts and socks
Nylon anorak for evenings
Small screwdriver and the more essential allen keys

A camping trip (more about that later)

Everything above (except the hair dryer), plus:
Tent and sleeping-bag
Cooking stove (once paraffin but now gas)
Lightweight pans
Plastic containers for food
Knife, fork and spoon
Tin opener and knife
Washing-up gear
Light to use inside tent (usually the bike's front light)
Under-mat for sleeping-bag
Cup
Fold-up water container
Matches
I often also take a book and a small radio

Saddle Bags

My first weekend away was to Oxford and Streatley youth hostels. I
carried my luggage in a duffel bag. The string cut my shoulders in the
first ten miles and I was extremely miserable until I bought a saddlebag. Never carry anything heavier than a camera on your shoulders.
Never, least of all, hump a rucksack. If you wonder why, just look at
rucksack carriers wobbling unhappily, their bent backs aching, their
balance threatened by the wash of every passing lorry.

A saddlebag holds all you need for a weekend. Put any overflow
into a handlebar bag and then into panniers beside the front wheel or
at the back. Front panniers distribute the load, especially on low
frames, but they make steering heavier. Rear panniers feel stable but
load the back wheel, which isn't good if you're not a lightweight. The

Front supports let you carry small panniers by the front wheel.
This is useful, but beware of the heavier steering.

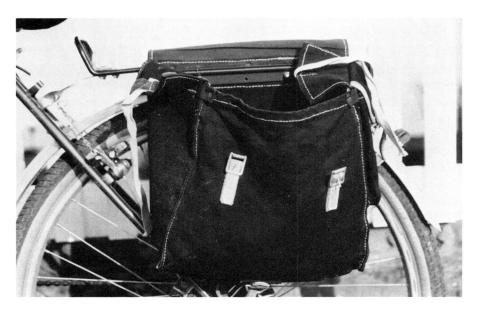

Traditional black cotton is the strongest material for bags, but it's
heavy, particularly in the rain.

Bike bags take a real hammering. Traditional canvas is almost indestructible, and it keeps its shape whether it's packed or empty, but it's heavier. Whatever the material, look for strong, simple fixings – this bag has double straps and a top that folds back for smaller loads. (Picture: Carradice)

spokes take extra weight and, as they wear loose, they break. One broken spoke is an irritation, but two or three mean a wobbling wheel that rubs on the mudguard and chain stays. British cyclists stay in love with their saddle bags, but their Continental cousins prefer panniers.

Rule 14 *Whatever you buy, get the biggest.*

Modern bags are nylon. It's lighter and more waterproof than black canvas. On the other hand, it wears more quickly, especially where it scrapes against a café or shop. It also holds its shape less, so that it droops over its rack. Also, remember that whatever the makers say, there's no such thing as a waterproof bag. Nylon bags have a draw-string, which helps, but line the bag with a plastic bag and then wrap your belongings into individual bags inside that. You won't regret it when the rain falls all day. And the bags will separate wet from dry when you repack.

Handlebar bags demand mechanical ingenuity in attaching their interlocking mounts but they're ideal for everyday bits and pieces and far better than carrying luggage on your back.

Ready for the road – not a racer, not even a super-lightweight; just an everyday bike prepared for a great holiday.

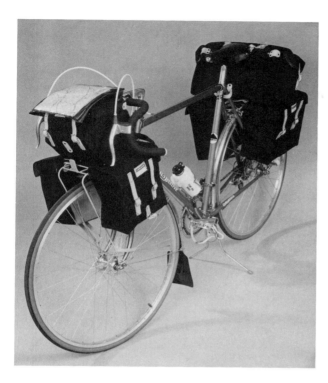

The trick is to carry it on your bike, not on your body. Spread the load around the bike, front and back. These are Carradice bags in traditional material.

A rear rack is essential. If the bag doesn't rub on the mudguard when you set off, it will later. Result: the mudguard rubs against the wheel and breaks. A rack also means you can carry panniers, which are roomier and in some ways better. They keep the load lower and you can separate what you need during the day from what can stay until night. You can keep food on one side and clothes on the other.

Divide your kit into groups. Anything you need during the day should stay near the top. Your tent should also be at the top so you can put it up in a shower without pulling out everything else first. And your waterproofs should also be accessible without having to open any bags at all.

Milometers, etc

You never ride as far when you're camping, perhaps only half to three-quarters of the normal distance. Once all you needed to know how far you'd ridden was a pin bolted to a spoke which struck a star wheel on a milometer mounted on the front forks. It made a click which became depressingly slower in headwinds and hills – and nobody really knew how accurate it was. Then came a quiet, belt-driven version and finally the electronic computer. You can now calculate your overall and trip distance to a metre, your actual, maximum and average speeds, your riding time, your crank-revolution frequency and your pulse rate, all with a gadget smaller than a matchbox.

The more you pay, the better gadget you get. The cheapest tell you only overall and trip distance, time of day and a few other things – which might be all you need. But electronics are seductive and you'll soon be looking at versions which tell you more but don't need wires running down your forks. These things become obsessive. You can also buy altimeters, total-ascent calculators, inclinometers and much else. You might conclude that you don't need them.

The star wheel took four minutes to fix. All you needed was the right model for the wheel. Computers, however, take more time. To get them right needs two people – you to sit on your bike to compress the tyre and someone else to measure the wheel and now-squashed tyre.

Whatever you buy, take care it's waterproof. Many people fit plastic bags over their meters when it's raining. There were certainly problems with the first imports, which came from California where rain is scarce. And another hint: either buy a model which *can't* be removed, or remove it whenever you leave the bike. If you have a model which calculates total average riding speed, put it in your pocket when you stop. It is depressing to sit with it on a café table, watching the average tumble by the minute.

7

Under the Stars

There's something special about camping. It goes back to why you started cycling: to escape petrol-driven, commerce-inspired life. Not that camping's disconnected from commerce, because lightweight tents aren't cheap. You have to work out the savings, financial and moral, multiply them by the number of camping holidays and calculate whether you end up with a profit. You also have to remember that, however light the equipment, you'll never crest hills with freshness. Bikepacking doesn't mean slogging, though. If it did I'd never do it. But it means gearing down, careful packing, specialist panniers, stronger spokes and acceptance that life will be a few miles an hour slower. The reward is to sleep in silence and solitude.

The world sends campers to organized sites, but that's for people with bungalow tents in car boots or trailers. My smallest tent is dark green, invisible after dusk, and too shallow to sit upright in. I once spent anxious moments in a field in France where *gamins* turned up for motorcycle practice. Fearful I'd be squashed by a passing Honda, I turned on a torch, scaring them with an eery green glow where there'd been only darkness.

Be responsible. All land is private. Make an effort to ask permission, though of course the countryside isn't full of signs saying 'This land is owned by the people in the big house a quarter of a mile back the way you've just come'. So use discretion. I don't cook in brittle, dry countryside (in fact I don't camp there full stop, because it's unreasonable to expect those who stand to lose their land and maybe their lives to know I have the sense not to light my stove). I don't camp on crops. But I do often camp in copses at field corners. The best 'wild' camping is in the north and north-west, in Wales and in Scotland and Ireland. Too much land in the south is crops, and the south, especially around London, can be too crowded. All the same, there's always somewhere. If you're stuck, look for signs erected by caravanners. Big sites are misery but small ones often have only one or two vans out of season and you'll sleep as well as anywhere, and you can have a wash and perhaps even launder your clothes as well.

> **Rule 15** *Beware cows, which are stupid and inquisitive. They come looking for you after you've turned in. They're uncaring and short-sighted and walk over your tent.*

Look for a site sheltered from the wind, or pitch with the stream-lined end of the tent into the breeze. Keep away from water, which can flood and attracts gnats. Don't camp under lone trees in thunder-storms or under any trees if you're nervous about branches falling in the night. Keep your head highest or you'll have a headache in the morning; and pitch in line with the hill and not across the slope, or you might find yourself in a mess of tent, bag and guy lines at the bottom of the valley. I love pine forests, for the scent and the carpet of needles. They can be cold but they don't drip as long as deciduous woods. They can be dark, even by daylight, which is fine for hiding the tent but is one reason why they're cold.

With a long chain, you can lock your bike to a pine, which you'll never do with an oak. There's no sure way to keep your bike safe, but nobody's likely to be around to steal it. Why pinch a bike in a field if you can steal one in town? And who knows it's there anyway? I lay it on the ground and loop the chain round the guy ropes or a tent pole. A horizontal bike is harder to see and take quietly. Other people say water will get into bearings and that nobody will see it upright any-way. Their trick is to loop string around the top tube and peg each end to the ground.

I ride for an hour towards the end of the day looking out for likely sites. They're not always obvious. When I've found one, I ride into the next village to buy food. I have a pint at the pub and use the loo sink for a wash. I fill my bottles with drinking water and, if I can, the fold-ing container that holds 1½ gallons and has a tap at the bottom. I balance that on the pannier carrier and ride back. Then I set up my tent.

Choosing a Tent

Never sleep in a tent which has just one skin. Either it's not waterproof and you'll get wet, or it is and you'll drown in condensation. Use the gap between the inner and outer skins. The more air that passes, the dryer you'll be. The gap can store bottles, stove and shoes. More than that, two skins let you use the outer to shelter if the weather turns bad

Once tents were only ridge if they were small or bell if they were for a whole army. Now internal hoops make them, like this Vango Discovery, into all sorts of roomy and interesting shapes.

during the day and the inner by itself at night if you're convinced it'll stay warm and dry.

Rule 16 *Choose a tent with one or two bell ends.*

Why? Well, you've got gear to store and there's never room in the tent, even assuming you want dirty panniers inside with you. When a manufacturer calls a tent two-man he means one-man, since tent manufacturers are rarely more than 4ft 6in or 5 stone. A one-man tent has the homeliness of an Egyptian mummy. There's a lot to be said for it, but space isn't one. Choose with baggage in mind. The bell also lets you sit in fresh air without getting more than a little wet from the rain. In many tents, it might be the *only* area to sit upright. If that sounds daft, it's because a lightweight tent is to sleep in and carry, not to spend whole days in and struggling to lift.

A porch, or bell end, gives you room for luggage and food.
(Picture by Vango)

Textbooks say never to cook in the bell, and I repeat the warning because doubtless you, too, have a solicitor. But even the most sensible campers have cooked in a pinned-back bell when the wind's howling and rain's falling. I've never found what else you can do. But be careful. Never *ever* do it close to the tent skin, and never cook in the shelter just because you can't be bothered to get out of your bag. If the weather's that bad, heat water for tea and a wash and escape to the nearest café for breakfast.

Nylon tents are the only choice. Cotton takes for ever to dry and weighs a ton when it's wet. The best nylon is Ripstop, which does as it says. Silicon isn't perfectly waterproof, which polyurethane is, but polyurethane weakens your tent, which is why it comes on cheaper, heavier and therefore stronger materials. If you want to be truly water-proof, the answer is PVC, but you'll rupture yourself lifting the tent.

Pure waterproofing is less crucial than you'd expect. Rain sheets down the outer skin. Passing through the pores of the fabric, especially when they're already water-filled, is a harder route. What goes through runs down the inside of the skin, provided it's not sagging or strung at too shallow an angle.

A tent's structure is governed by its supports. Some string it up from a bike propped or pegged against a tree. But the usual choice is poles or hoops. Poles give you an approximate triangle – the exact shape depends on the design – and hoops give you a pipe or igloo. Poles are simpler and lighter but your tent rises to a narrow ridge and the outer can be less stressed and therefore potentially less waterproof. It also catches the wind. Hoops sit inside the fabric and hold it upright and expanded by trying to straighten themselves against the tent. Winter ramblers like hooped tents because they survive snow on a mountainside, but the luxury of cycling is being able to ride to a spot in the valley. The best option is a pole tent in which the pole at the higher end (usually the door, because lightweight tents rise from head to toe as well as from ground to ridge) is replaced by two poles in an inverted V, giving unobstructed access. Make sure the poles fold enough to fit your bags.

Aim for a tent that weighs 1kg per person and never more than 2kg. One-man tents are proportionately heavier – perhaps only a kilo lighter than a two-man – because a little tent has as many ropes and things as a big one. But from two-man upwards, the 1–2kg guide works well. The larger the tent, the closer it should be to 1kg. Makers' weights are optimistic – so much so that some shops weigh tents and list their own results rather than the makers'.

Make sure that the outer skin can be erected before the inner. It's good to have the choice – inner or outer first – but pegging out the vulnerable, unwaterproofed inner first won't appeal in a deluge. You might not get the choice, especially with hooped tents. Then you have to ask yourself how often you expect to camp in the rain, how frequently you'll move on during your holiday, and how far away the next tent shop is. Never buy a tent you can't put up in the dark.

Other things to check:
- that the door zips run the height of the tent and operate from both ends
- that the bottoms of the tent (the brails) roll up to ventilate the tent
- that the guys are partially rubber or elastic, so tightening in the rain or wind doesn't tug the tent.

Cooking

How much you cook depends on your mood and where you're camping. Some people love boiling potatoes and frying sausages beside a stream; others prefer food cooked for them. If nothing else, you'll want hot water to wash and make tea, so you'll need a stove. I used a paraffin stove for years because paraffin was easy to carry and burned furiously and cheaply. There was the fiddle of pumping the pressure and priming the jet with tablets that burned and went out, and now and again you could produce a conflagration fit for Pudding Lane, but it was The Real Thing. Then I took it to Holland and it was impossible to buy paraffin or priming tablets. My friend Maurice told me I should have bought a petrol stove; they're simpler, he kept saying, and you can buy petrol anywhere. They were also safer, although when you got one really wrong you needed Red Adair. But by then I'd bought bottled gas.

I don't like the waste of empty canisters, and I'm never convinced they're not leaking. Nor do I like not seeing how much gas is left. But that's life – never perfect. At least gas bottles are on sale everywhere. The alternative is a pan set called Trangia, which burns meths, which you can buy by the half-pint at hardware shops, but it's not as easy to get as petrol, although the pans work beautifully and fold into the largest container.

High in the hills you need dehydrated food if you're away from shops for a couple of days, and then you'll need water to reconstitute it. Fortunately, wild-country streams tumble over rocks and burst and bubble and purify themselves. I wouldn't drink peat water, and I walk upstream to reassure myself there are neither dead sheep in the water nor small boys relieving themselves, but I don't go to much more trouble than that. You could always use water purifying tablets.

Sleeping-Bags

Word was that you had to have down or you'd shiver. Now there must be fewer ducks, because down bags are formidably expensive. You could stay a fortnight in a hotel for less. The ones you see are a mixture of down and synthetic material, and the cheaper bags are synthetic, which isn't bad for warmth but bulkier and heavier. You'll roll a down bag to 20 x 30cm, but never an artificial one.

The makers have the same view about weather as tent makers have about people. While all campers are midgets, so everyone is resilient to cold. Bags grade by season: two-season, three-season and so on. This means nothing, since it can be warm in the Highlands and snowing in Kent. Much also depends on the insulation between you and the ground – a polystyrene sheet like a Karrimat is warmer, if harder, than an air bag, and newspaper will make it still warmer – and on the quality of your tent. TOG numbers appear on bags as they do on duvets, but your best advice comes from the man in the shop. Look for a rambling and mountaineering specialist, a man who knows there's more to camping than the Sunnyside Caravan and Camping Site.

Pick a bag with no or only a short zip; which has a hood into which the bag can roll and which will act as a stuff-sack for a pillow; in which insulation is sewn into panels rather than left to fall into heaps at the end and sides; that's tapered towards the toes to save space and warmth. Some bags have padded hoods that you push your head into, so that you feel warm at the expense of looking like a nasty bug. I can't tell you how they work, but if I tossed and turned, I'd worry I'd unscrew my head at the neck.

Bags are hard to wash. Some people say you never should, especially down bags, because they're never the same. Even artificial bags take for ever to dry. If you do, use specialist soap, not commercial detergent or soap. Never use a washing machine. There's not much you can do to keep the outside pristine, save keep the tent swept, but you can preserve the inside with a sheet liner which can be washed. Make your own, so that it tapers with the bag.

Before you pack for the morning, drag your bag into the dry, pump it to reloft the packing, and hang it to air. Then roll it up and pack it away. Take the tent down, keep the inner dry and put the tent pegs in a heap. One lost peg's not a disaster, but every subsequent one will be. Pack your tent into the top of one pannier, roll your insulation sheet into a dustbin liner and strap it across your luggage, push your bike down to the road . . . and another day has started.

8

Of Nuts and Bolts

And so we come to the bike itself. I'm not going back on my claim that any bike will do, that all you have to do is get on and ride. But there are two additional truths: a bike that falls to bits is a bike that falls to bits; some bikes are better than others. Going for a ride takes you away from spanners, screwdrivers and puncture patches. You could take everything with you, but if fun is taking a bike to bits then you'd have a better time as a bike-shop mechanic. A bike should give you minimum grief. It's just a way of interpreting your love of gentle travel. If it doesn't do that, it's a hell of a nuisance.

There's no shortage of simple and expensive grease and oil for your bike – the trick is to remember to use it. In winter, a thin coat of car engine oil sticks to the chain better than lighter oil.

All the tools you need for a few days away – a sachet of oil,
puncture patches and repair solution, tyre levers, screwdriver,
chain riveter, spoke key, spare brake or gear cable, spare spoke,
adjustable spanner.

Saddles

> **Rule 17** *Make sure you are as comfortable as possible and pushing on the pedals as much as possible.*

I met a chap called Henri Christiaans once. He's a boffin at the technical university in Delft, where the pottery comes from, in Holland. He'd just conducted a survey into saddles and bottoms. Bikes, like shoes, are forgiving. It's surprising how far you can walk in somebody else's boots. But in the end it's better to have a pair of soft leather that follow the shape of your feet. For boots, read saddle. Henri had probably never read *Three Men on the Bummel*, but he'd have been interested. One character says: 'There may be a better land where bicycle saddles are made out of rainbow stuffed with cloud, [but] in this world the simplest thing is to get used to something hard.' Even old friends can let you down. Johnny Helms once pictured a cyclist peering mystified at the perfectly ordinary outline of his saddle, rubbing his backside. 'Ah,' says another cyclist, 'I once had a saddle like that as well.'

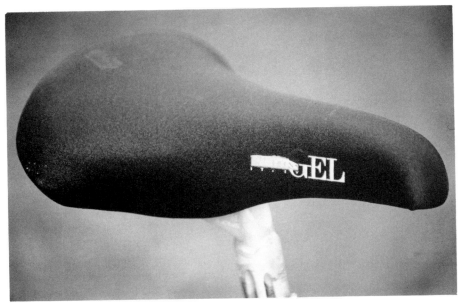

Saddles were once made of leather. Technology has brought firm but soft surfaces, often with gel pads to pamper the bones. Wider widths with shorter noses, like this one, are now available for women.

It's odd that folk take so little care in choosing a saddle. Christiaans said if shops sold bikes *without* saddles, buyers and shops would spend more time considering what to sit on. As it was, millions took it for granted that a saddle would be uncomfortable. The consequences are severe. Of the 900 that Christiaans and his helpers stopped, men complained of sore seat bones, numb penis, and a sore perineum (the skin in vertical contact with the saddle); women had sore seat bones and tailbones (from sitting more upright) and irritation and even damage to the genitals and the surrounding skin.

Some had tried a new saddle, others had made adjustments. A few had varied their clothes or tried creams. But nothing worked well. Christiaans took six for more tests. The changes they'd made had been haphazard. They never put their saddles at the right height. Women were too embarrassed to inquire at bike shops and, if they went to a doctor, they understandably presented themselves and not the bicycle. He set the order of adjustments. First the type of saddle, then its height, then its forward–backward position and the angle of the nose, and then the geometry of the frame.

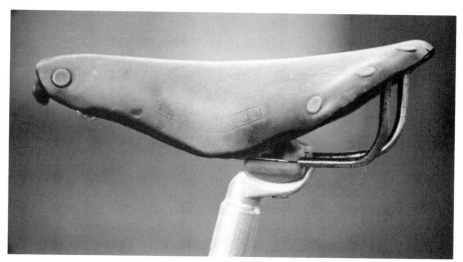

Saddles come in many materials but nothing lasts longer or moulds to you better than leather. In days long gone, riders kept their saddles when they changed their bikes. This Brooks Professional, soaked in neatsfoot oil and carved at the edges when new, is still going strong after two decades.

Another veteran saddle. The Unica was the first plastic saddle. It was comfortable and light if slippery. This one has survived because, unlike most saddles, it shrugs at the rain. A soaking will spoil a leather saddle and ruin many modern composite ones.

The saddle must support the main bones without flaring and rubbing the legs as well. It must make you feel comfortable without being sprung and giving way as you pedal. The nose mustn't be too long, too hard or raised. Push on the top and see if the cheeks flare. If it's a bad case, the top will be so bashed that the cheeks are like the splayed legs of a dead beetle. This is what the trade calls A Hopeless Case – nothing to be done, it'll wear your legs raw. Look under the nose of the saddle. If there's a nut and bolt, find a spanner that'll fit the nut and the limited space around it and turn so that the thread pushes the nose out. The saddle cover should follow and draw the cheeks in. Make a few turns a day.

If it's a leather saddle, grease the *underside* with a teaspoon of neatsfoot oil. The leather will soften and eventually pull itself into shape. But many saddles, particularly old ones, are a compromise. Very old leather saddles had big coiled springs at the back but otherwise followed the principles of adjustable tension. But later saddle makers discovered that *(a)* leather was expensive and difficult to craft, and *(b)* it was cheaper and appeared more comfortable to make saddles with an artificial surface and a network of springs like a mattress. These saddles can not be adjusted. Sorry.

Here you discover why committed cyclists ride hard, narrow, unsprung saddles. Leather has given way to plastics but the hardness

Never tilt the nose of the saddle down or more than fractionally up. If you have to tilt it, you've got your overall riding position wrong. Start again.

prevents splaying, the narrowness ends leg friction, and the absence of springs means every erg gets to the pedals instead of compressing the springs.

> **Rule 18** *Take time over buying. Expect to see all the shop has.*

You'll sit on your saddle for a long time. Science offers gel pads and heaven knows what else. There are women's saddles, with broader beams and narrower noses. And while I prefer leather, because I'm a fogey and nothing beats leather *once you've broken it in*, the world in general revels in the lightness and design of plastic. Never buy from a bike shop that sells Esso Blue, hammers, model toys and skateboards. Buy from a shop that knows the business. And if you have an experienced cyclist as a friend, borrow his unused saddles (most cyclists have one or two) and learn the different effects they have.

Fitting

Fit the saddle horizontal and in the middle of the underframe. Tighten the bolt and then slacken the bolt or allen key that clamps the seat pin in the frame. Pull the pin right out, which is the only way to see how long it is, and give the lower half a smear of heavy grease. That'll stop it welding itself to the frame next winter.

Put it back so that two inches are inside the frame. Never have less than two inches. If the saddle's now too low, you'll have to buy either a longer seatpin (difficult but inexpensive) or a new frame (easy but costly). With luck it'll be too high, in which case push it down until it looks about right and then tighten it. Sit on the saddle, take off your shoes, push one pedal as far away as it'll go, and put your *heels* on the pedals. Turn gently backwards. Can you do it without the slightest rocking on the saddle? If you can, raise the saddle half an inch. Carry on raising it until pedalling forces you to rock slightly, then lower the saddle a quarter of an inch, tighten it and you have the right up-and-down position.

That's your bottom sorted out. Your knees are next. Put your shoes back on, place the pedals horizontal and put the ball of your foot above the axle. Is the groove at the back of your kneecap now directly above the axle? If it isn't, slacken the bolt that fixes the saddle to the pin and slide the saddle until it's right. There should usually be enough adjustment, but you might have trouble if you're taller or shorter than average. In that case you'll need a longer underframe, or

Place the ball of your foot exactly over the pedal spindle.

Raise or lower your saddle so that a slight bend remains in your leg.

Move the saddle until your knee is above the pedal when the crank is horizontal.

an old-fashioned nut-and-ratchet seatpin to turn back-to-front to move the saddle further forward. When you've got the right position, make the saddle horizontal again and lock it in place. And that's the job done.

If the saddle's too high you'll get a sore backside; if it's too low, your legs will ache and you might damage your knees; if it's too far forward or back, your back will ache as well. There'll always be some sort of ache when you start anyway. But believe me – it doesn't last.

Saddle sores type one are bruising. Nature gave you a hollow in your bottom between the two main bones, the ischials, that poke through to the chair you're sitting on. It's not accustomed to being dropped on to a hard saddle. Next day you'll feel like someone's been round your backside with a steam-hammer. But take heart! This bruising will (a) go, and (b) after a few minutes of cycling again you won't feel it (the Hair of the Dog school of cycling, this), and (c) after a handful of rides you'll never feel it again – provided you keep cycling two or three times a week, almost regardless of distance.

Saddle sores type two are more sinister. They're genuine soreness, even red irritation, rather than ache. They're caused by friction. So, Sherlock, if not the saddle then where do they come from? It might be your clothing. Dinky shorts which don't separate your thighs from the saddle will let your legs rub raw. Answer: longer, thicker shorts. Jeans are too tight, another cause. The friction might be imperceptible but, repeated several thousand times, it's like a Surform. Thick baggy trousers, knickers with seams and gussets – almost anything might be the culprit.

And since I don't propose inspecting your loin arrangements myself, you're on your own. Try proper cycling shorts (not the flimsy fashion version), or a soft tracksuit, even conventional but slightly longer shorts. Once cured, the problem won't recur.

Handlebars

Now set your handlebars. For anything apart from pottering to shops, handlebars should never be higher than your saddle. Weight makes

Place the handlebars lower than the saddle – the taller you are the greater will be the gap – and fit a handlebar extension if necessary to achieve an effect similar to that shown here.

The result is a mechanically efficient, even balance in a casual riding position . . .

. . . and a comfortable but streamlined shape for headwinds, fast riding and descents.

the caster effect keep the front wheel straight. Take the weight off and you're effectively riding no-hands; yes, you can do it, but you don't spend all day doing it.

There are many theories about handlebars but they go to pieces because people come in different shapes and use their bikes for different things. One says bars should be no further from the peak of your saddle than the length of your forearm. Why, I don't know, and I've never possessed a bike where this is so. Certainly, if you have the bars too close you'll ride too heavily on the saddle and your steering will feel too light. And if you have them too far away, your back will ache and you'll have too much weight on your arms instead of the saddle. So it's a compromise.

Most experienced riders have it right and if you keep your eyes open you'll know what's right. If it looks right, it usually is. The taller you are, the greater the vertical difference between your handlebars (lower) and the saddle (higher), but it can't be otherwise mechanically anyway. You can only get the handlebars so far out of the frame. And the longer your arms and back, the longer the extension you'll need to push the handlebars away, but that's also logical because the placing of the saddle is fixed by the length of your thighs and the position of your pedals. In the end, for all you fiddle, if the frame's too big or small, it's too big or small. You can only do what you'd do with that pair of shoes: throw, sell or exchange. Fortunately, a bike's highly adjustable so you're deeply unlucky or just plain miserly if it doesn't come right.

Mountain bike fans claim they get more control from entirely straight handlebars.

To adjust handlebar height or alignment, use a spanner or allen key to slacken the expansion bolt inside the stem . . .

. . . turn it until it rises clear of the surface . . .

. . . protect the surface with a cloth . . .

. . . and knock it down flat with a hammer.

Now hold the wheel between your legs and raise, lower and straighten the handlebars.

Finally, retighten the handlebars securely.

Brakes

Now try the brakes. They should work smoothly, on and off. The pads should be healthy, and the right way round. The right way round is with the shoe, which holds the block, enclosed at the forward end so the rims don't send the blocks flying loose. Polished steel rims are scary in the rain – where is the logic of chroming surfaces which rely on friction? You can change the wheels, which is expensive but will lessen the revolving weight and make the bike easier to ride, or you can change the blocks.

Try softer rubber, of the sort used on aluminium rims. Try them carefully and see whether there's an improvement. If there is, stick with them but remember that they'll wear more quickly. Hunt out a shop which sells blocks without shoes as well. Adjust the shoes so that the blocks come tight and level with the rim. A small nut does the trick. Now inspect the cable. Pull the lever and peer inside; the slightest fraying is dangerous. Now look at the other end; if that's also frayed, it's not dangerous but it *is* a nuisance because frayed cable won't go through the clamp. Brake cables aren't expensive, so replace them.

Service the brakes by unclamping the cables and pulling them out,

Centre-pull brakes – almost standard on mountain bikes – are just the revival of a very old idea. They look clumsy but they give better leverage when the bike's loaded.

Check the cable inside the brake levers by pulling on the brake and peering inside. Change the cable at the first sign of fraying. And tug hard – better to break it before you leave than out on the road.

remembering how they sat inside the levers. Grease them and thread them back into the cover. Retighten so that only minimal leverage pulls the blocks to the rim. This job takes three hands – one to force the brake to the rim, one to pull the cable, the third to tighten the nut.

How tight you get the brakes depends on your skill and your wheels. A small wobble is normal in cheap wheels, but quality wheels should run true. Test the brakes repeatedly. At the most innocent, you might pull the cable more tautly through the outer, so that you have to retighten it. But at the most sinister, you'll find you haven't seated the cable at the lever, so that it comes loose, or that you didn't tighten the nut at the brake end, so that it pulls through. Or the cable snaps. Better you break something in your garage than on the road.

The usual problem is that brakes won't release evenly. The Pedal Cycles (Construction and Use) Regulations 1983 have plenty to say about having the required number of brakes but nothing about how well they must work, which is a shame. Cheap brakes are poorly made.

One side leaves the rim and the other sticks. They work when they leave the factory but never after you've adjusted them. The more you pay, the better they work, which is consoling as you write out the cheque.

Alignment is by a spring at the back, which can be fiddled with a screwdriver and pliers. This assumes that the pivot on which the brake arms move isn't solid with dirt and grease. Quality brakes adjust with an allen key and the time will come when you realize the price is well worth it.

The brakes, by the way, look the same but work differently. Contrary to what your teacher or the policeman at the cycling proficiency examinations said, it's the front brake that's for everyday use and not the back. People who've never ridden a bike in a decade or more are strong on tales of the front brake sending you over the handlebars at the slightest application. Would that they were that efficient.

The front brake will stop you solidly and efficiently. It might even throw your weight forward on to your arms more than you expected. But you will stop. Deceleration throws your weight forward and therefore off the back wheel. The reduced weight at the back means back-tyre traction is less, which means a skid until you learn the trick of keeping your weight back above the saddle. Since the skid can't go forwards, the energy gets dissipated sideways and the back of the bike breaks away and you fall off.

> **Rule 19** *Use both brakes, either together or with the back fractionally before the front.*

Take care using either brake on wet or greasy roads. The knack comes quickly, but it has to be acquired. In principle it's better to do as you would in a car and brake before a corner and not during it. If you're forced to brake during the corner, the bike will start falling inwards because the centrifugal force has been reduced. The urge to pull the bike upright is automatic. Use both brakes every so often if you want to control your speed on a long descent. Don't keep them on all the time – there's just the chance (a certainty on Alpine descents) that you'll heat the rims and your inner tube will blow.

Wheels and Tyres

Wheels true by turning the nipples, at the rim end of the spokes. It's not for amateurs. Many can do it, but I chase the buckle round the wheel. The spokes are then different tensions and break a few hundred miles later. A spoke key (a nipple spanner) is a wise investment as are a handful of spokes of the right size in case you break some on tour; but beyond emergency repairs (difficult, when the spoke breaks on the gear side of the back wheel), I leave spoke jobs to a bike shop.

And the tyres? They should have as much tread as they're supposed to have. The narrowest have scarcely any. They're so narrow that water can't build up, so tread isn't needed. The reasoning works well, but narrow tyres aren't appropriate for loaded bikes. They wear too quickly because the pressure is too concentrated. Mountain-bike tyres go to the other extreme (although, quaintly, there are now slicks for mountain-bike riders who never want to leave streets), with chunky treads to grip and dispose of the mud. Butyl inner tubes hold air better but give a heavier ride; they also stick to puncture patches less easily. Natural rubber is coming back, at a price. They need topping up every morning, but the ride is livelier.

 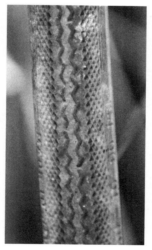 

High-pressure tyres (left) often have only slight treads. With such a narrow profile and so little of the tyre on the road, that's all that's needed. Heavier treads (centre) are needed for everyday riding, though, and heavier still (right) for loaded touring. The wider base gives a softer ride, the thicker rubber makes punctures slightly less likely, and the zig-zag tread is needed to carry road water away from the wider surface.

Get a good pump. Everyday bikes have Schraeder, car-style valves, to fit foot-pumps and, less safe, compressed air lines. That's useful and easier, although air lines overpump low-pressure tyres (with warnings from safety people each year about blowing a poorly fitted tyre off the rim) or they can't cope with the 100psi and more that lightweight tyres demand.

Car-style valves also leak at high pressure. Experienced riders prefer narrower, Presta valves with small pistons inside. The pump forces air around the piston into the tube. As the pump pressure falls, the trapped air pushes the valve shut again. When the pressure's right, all you have to do is screw the fixing nut tight to stop the valve opening inadvertently.

How do you know whether the tyre's at the right pressure? What *is*

A stirrup pump in appearance, but known as a track pump. Open the tyre valve, push the end of the hose over it, check that the rubber washers hold it in place, and start pumping. High pressures come far more easily than with a handpump.

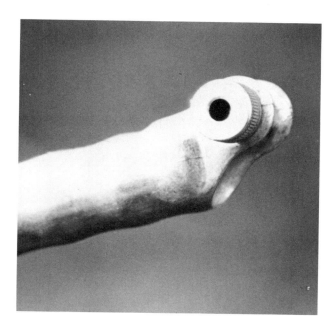

Good pumps have press-on connectors instead of the traditional few centimetres of rubber hose. The direct link between pump and valve means higher pressures and no lost effort. Takes a bit of practice but, once you've perfected it, you'll never go back.

the right pressure? Well, the strange position of the second governs the way you do the first. All tyres have a pressure printed on their side, but I discovered some years ago that the same make and class of tyre can have different pressures in different countries. I have no idea why, and I recall the CTC's technical people looking into it. The only universal truth is that tyres should be pumped hard, so that there's just the slightest give in the *sidewalls*. Pressing the tread is pointless.

Nobody enjoys pumping. The hardest way is to use a duff pump that generates no pressure. The next hardest is to use a decent pump with a screw-on connector, because it leaks and expands enough with each puff to take some of the air out of your efforts. The best hand-pumps have press-on adaptors built into the end; you unlock the valve, push the adaptor over it, and pump away. Press-on adaptors usually fit only Presta valves. That's the sort of pump to take with you. At home, treat yourself to a workshop stirrup-pump which generates high pressures easily. Push the hose on to the valve and pump, watching the meter rise. Feel the tyre until you're happy, note the pressure, and remember it. Narrow, sporty tyres take 90–100psi, sports bikes and roadsters are around 65–90psi.

It's unlikely you'll do any damage by overpumping, unless you do it dramatically, but under-pumping ruins sidewalls, wears tyres and

*Pump tyres until the walls have only the slightest give. The
figures printed on the sidewalls vary from country to country, so
they're only a guide. Most pumps have a red area to stop you
going far too far, and some – like this one – have an adjustable red
needle to set at your own tyres' maximum.*

makes it hard work to ride. The less tyre on the road, the less resistance. Soft tyres spread side to side and fore and aft as well. You're
perpetually pushing spongy rubber ahead of you.

Lights

Now you're ready to go – by day, anyway. In all but midsummer, it's
wise to leave your lights on the bike. You never know when you'll be
out at dusk; and why rush home just because the light's fading when
the only price to pay is the pound or two that lights weigh?

But what lights? At first there were bobby-dodgers, which met
the law because the law said little about what a light should do. In
fact, when back lights were first imposed they met resistance from
the cycling establishment. The argument was that they took from the

Good lights are essential. The front light on the left is American and has a halogen bulb that casts more light than the lens area suggests; the light on the right is British and a great improvement on older versions.

overtaker (a driver with headlights) responsibility for avoiding things in his way. Before long, protestors argued, motorists would insist that a mown-down cyclist had brought the accident on himself by not making himself visible. And motorists, they argued, would drive faster than their headlamps allowed knowing 'it was for cyclists to make themselves obvious and get out of the way.'

Even today, when the battle is forgotten, many motorcyclists turn on their headlamps in daylight with the same heavy heart. The bike rider's problems come not simply from enemies but friends. Bike lights are restricted by the pea-brained attitude of makers and now and again by the law. At least we are out of the era when lights just did not stay alight, couldn't be fitted without toestraps, and rattled unless wedged with newspaper. Only when cyclists turned to French lights which were brighter and dependable – even though they didn't reach the British Standard on which the law insisted – did British lamp makers wake up.

'Would any motor manufacturer ever dare,' Peter Knottley asked, 'to produce beautifully made cars and expect no one to complain when the lights went out and then dropped off?'

The situation, then, is this: you must have a white light in front and red to the rear all through lighting-up times. You must also have a red rear reflector, which can be part of the rear lamp. There are British Standards for lights and reflectors. Unlike a motorist, a cyclist doesn't have to carry lights during the day. Flashing lights other than turning indicators (novel, but useless) are illegal. They're on sale and you might even think they're good sense, but the law says you can't use them. Your lights must be fixed to the bike. It's not even certain whether it's legal to fix a light to a rolled-up cape strapped beneath the saddle. I don't think anybody would contest the point, but the law does say 'to the bike'.

Most riders use battery lights. Dynamos are brighter and cheaper to operate, but they're heavier, fiddlier, they can't be removed simply and they drag (unless you have one of the now obsolete hub dynamos, which work immaculately without effort). They also go out when you stop, and faster riders blow the bulbs (beaten by fitting overrated ones). I have a love-hate relationship with dynamos, which at decent speeds cast a brilliant light quite clear enough to persuade motorists to dip theirs, but which drag on the wheel. My greatest complaint was that the bulbs blew so easily since the makers can't find a compromise between something that burns at low speeds yet which doesn't over-load when driven harder.

This all changed when my wife, who is electronically aware and knows what to ask for in shops that sell valves and diodes and bits of old wire, bought me a little black box about the size of a square of chocolate. The wires go in one side and come out the other. Quite what happens inside I've never discovered, except that the effect is that all the surplus electricity disappears and the bulbs stay alight.

I still get the odd slip of the dynamo on wet tyres and I still carry spare bulbs just in case. And I still curse at the vulnerability and ugli-ness of the wiring, something made worse by my distrust of using the frame itself as the earth wire and my preference for a second length of cable instead. Earthing problems are the main reason that dynamos flicker. There are nights I swear I'll rip the whole lot off and hurl it into the canal, but when I think of all the batteries I'd have to buy and the weakness of battery lights, I change my mind. Now I've got a battery bike and a dynamo bike as a compromise.

I prefer sidewall dynamos to those that drive off the tread, by the way. Tread dynamos are neater and hide away between the chain-stays, but I find them unpredictable when rainwater is streaming down the tyre tread. So-called bottle dynamos – the sort that drive off the sidewall – are uglier but they get my vote. I fit them to rub at the very bottom of the track that's made for them on the tyre, rather than towards the circumference where rainwater gathers near the tread before being flung off.

It's a shame makers don't fit lights as standard. It would encourage more people to ride more of the day, and it might lessen drivers' complaints that too many cyclists ride without lights.

Reflectors

According to the law, any bike bought or first used since September 1985 has to have pedal reflectors front and back. The back is no problem with conventional pedals (although reflectors won't fit specialist

The law says your pedals must have reflectors fore and aft. The front is almost always impossible. The back can be bodged on traditional pedals like these and can work quite well, but clipless pedals are impossible.

Mudguards nearly always come with a legal reflector. You can treat yourself to a larger one, but you'll have to drill your own hole in the guards to fit it.

pedals) but the front proves impossible. Either there's nowhere to put it, or it squashes when you ride away with your foot on the bottom of the pedal (which you nearly always will). Bike makers, stuck with this law and the fact that nobody in Britain makes pedals in quantity, leave them to dealers to fit. The dealers can't do it either. The position gets dafter when you consider that front reflectors are hidden by your shoes. Few policemen (or anybody else) realize the law exists.

Dealers also have to fit spoke reflectors, but the law (for the moment) doesn't say you can't take them straight off again. Few experienced riders use them, first because they're not much use (who would sit in the middle of the road at night, at 90 degrees to traffic?) and second because they feel they unbalance the wheel. They also look nasty. If you insist on sideways reflection, use reflective tyres. At least they throw light at more than 90 degrees, which is better than pedal reflectors. Large mudguard reflectors are angled to a prism, which is helpful, but beyond that they're little better than an anachronism when used with a back light (which is bigger, brighter and by law has to be visible from the side).

Reflective tyres, with millions of glass fragments fixed to the side-walls, throw some light sideways. Few cycling accidents happen at 90 degrees, which is where reflective tyres do work extremely well. That,

Some tyres have millions of tiny glass beads set into a reflective rim beside the edge of the tread. They work well in some circumstances.

of course, is the angle that advertisements promote. But drivers are rarely at 90 degrees to or directly behind a cyclist (being closer to the off-side than the kerb-side of the road). Fit bike reflectors if you feel happier. But a good back light's better, and a Sam Browne reflective harness (which moulds with the body and reflects in more angles) is a useful addition.

Keeping Dry

There's no way to stay perfectly dry because rain seeps or blows from the outside or condenses on the inside. Cyclists have for years worn all-enveloping capes, normally yellow or orange plastic. They were a bodge at best and a nuisance in wind. They also never fitted any known human shape. You see fewer these days because they're harder to buy and because there are rainsuits on sale.

How good rainsuits are depends on what they're made of. Fabrics like Gore-Tex are advertised as allowing clammy air to pass from inside to outside without letting rain in. It's all to do with relative molecule size. *CT&C* fills with arguments – that suits are wonderful or an expensive waste. They're not cheap, over a hundred pounds more than a cape that costs little more than a tenner. Much depends on how fast you ride and how you sweat. There's no dispute they keep out the rain; the argument is whether they let out sweat and how well fabrics breathe when dirty. The labels are a gobbledygook of figures.

I'd rather not get wet, but I assume I will a bit because I've chosen an outdoor hobby. Whether from the inside or the outside seems hardly worth worrying about. A cape makes your back wet from *warm* perspiration and condensation, whereas the rain outside is cold. The shock comes when you remove it and release the tropical atmosphere inside it. The next couple of miles can prove chilly. Sit on the tail of your cape to stop it blowing, and hold the front or extend the thumb loops that the makers fit too short inside. That stops the front blowing up. Lift the front every so often; even if it doesn't change the fetid air, it makes you feel better for trying.

The French portray Britain as a nation under umbrellas, taking their pleasures sadly. It's not true. The area closest to France – eastern England – is so dry that water companies say it's in almost continuous drought. The west is wetter, but even there the rain falls in solid but infrequent lumps rather than Irish-style daily drizzle. And the chances of getting wet cycling both to and from work for a 9-to-5 day are slight.

Mudguards

You'll feel miserable if the rain your cape deflects is then thrown back by your tyres. Fit mudguards, with a healthy flap at the bottom of the front guard and, if you ride in company, a long extension to the back. It's bad enough being sprayed by your own tyres; having water chucked by someone else's gives you thoughts described as un-neighbourly.

Treat yourself to decent guards. They'll repay you well. Cheap ones with single stays on each side can wrap themselves around the wheel and fetch you off. Don't let the guards or their stays chatter on the tyre. Whether your foot snags on the front guard depends on your frame

Fit mudguards close and parallel to the tyre and cut short and trim the four bare ends of the mudguard stays with the plastic tips provided – it makes them safer for anyone who rides into you and falls on them.

and the size of your feet. Many riders manage well with a front wheel that won't turn if their cranks are horizontal – their feet wouldn't be there if they were taking a corner, they argue – but more find it unnerving. On small frames you might have no choice, although you could hunt for cranks shorter than the standard 170mm.

Helmets

Finally, consider a helmet. Should you wear one? Are they any good? How great are the sentimental and commercial lobbies? Assuming that all accidents are reported, 300 cyclists a year die in Britain and 100,000 are injured. Many suffer head injuries, but that means anything from a shaving nick to a fatal impact. Of the cyclists who die,

Wear a cycling helmet if you feel happier, but remember that they
don't do everything that popular sentiment credits them with.
And make sure it's light and well ventilated.

around 70 per cent have had a head injury. And there the argument is left in advertising. It doesn't follow that 210 cyclists would be alive each year (70 per cent of 300) if they'd worn helmets. Of the 300, many die from multiple injuries of which a head injury is only one. Many have been in collisions with cars and lorries, against which helmets are useless. Helmets protect in a fall but they do nothing if you're hit by a car.

The highest standard is the equivalent of a helmeted head falling 4ft 10in on concrete at 12mph, which is about right for a cyclist. But as the government's own statistics show, being hit at 35mph or more, whether as a cyclist or a pedestrian, is generally fatal. That doesn't mean helmets don't work at more than 12mph. They will, but only if another part of the body hits the ground first, slowing your head. Cyclists rarely land on top of their heads, and most cycling head injuries are just over the ears and eyes. Helmets, because you have to be able to see, don't protect these areas completely. Fortunately the road is flat so that the thickness of the helmet (not inconsiderable) helps.

The internal protection is never as good as a motorcycle helmet's, nor can the outer material be as strong or the helmet as all-enclosing. Ventilation and lightness for strenuous activity isn't a question for a motorcycle helmet. And even a motorcycle helmet will often not take a direct hit from a fast vehicle.

The CTC's view is neither to encourage nor discourage. Least of all does it want helmets made compulsory. It accepts they might help children 'playing' on bicycles (not a pejorative expression: the Traffic Road Research Laboratory says most children's accidents happen while playing or doing tricks); added to that, children have higher centres of gravity.

The cure – distraction, heat and limited visibility – can be worse than the ill. Wearing a helmet increases the reason for wearing one. And many people to whom cycling is an occasional ride to the library, might be put off cycling altogether if helmets became compulsory.

Australia was first to compel. The number of cyclists fell (resistance to wearing a helmet) but accidents rose. Statistics tell you anything, but these give the odd thought that many people would have had fewer accidents if they *hadn't* been wearing helmets. It was the *safe* riders who'd been put off cycling, and those who remained seemingly rode in more danger than before.

If helmets are to be worn, they should be good helmets and outrageous claims shouldn't appeal to sentiment and unfounded public fears. That's why the CTC helped form the British Standard in 1986. BS6863 is much the same as other countries'. Chris Juden says: 'I would not say that this is the last word in helmet standards. Many other countries have equally valid standards, some of which are in some ways preferable, while there are certainly parts of BS6863 which I think others would do well to copy.'

Most helmets sold here are made in America where the lobby is so strong that some publishers refuse pictures of riders without one. The American standard is ANSI z90.4. Juden says a helmet with this standard and one from the private Snell organization offers as much protection as you can get, adding: 'Fortunately some of the best-ventilated designs belong to this category – but they are also the most expensive.' Helmets meeting the British Standard have rarely been among the most comfortable he's tried. The Australian standard is AS2063, which Juden rates mid-way between ANSI and Snell. There will eventually be a European standard.

Price is not reflective of how well a helmet works, but you'd have to pay at least £65 (1994 price) to find one sufficiently ventilated. The cheapest have no ventilation at all.

Take care your helmet fits. Small, Medium or Large have no relevance. Have your head measured. Any discrepancy can usually be matched by the sponge pads inside the shell. The CTC, the Bicycle Association and the Association of Cycle Traders have a guide to helmets and what they will and won't do, and how to choose one. It's available from CTC headquarters. It was on the advice of the CTC that the draft of the 1992 Highway Code was changed to avoid misleading advice.

Problems

What happens if something goes wrong on the road? Punctures are the commonest problem, although infrequent. The trick is to carry a spare inner tube so that you can remove the punctured one and mend it later. And the routine is this:

1. Let the remaining air out of the tyre, unbolt the wheel and remove it. If it's the back wheel, change into top gear (the smallest sprocket) first.
2. Remove the lock ring on the inner tube.
3. Insert a tyre lever under the edge of the tyre somewhere opposite the valve and then another a few centimetres away from it; lever both down until a section of tyre comes clear of the rim. Remove all one side of the tyre so that it falls outside the rim while the other stays between the rim edges.
4. Pull out all the inner tube, working towards the valve, then push the valve up through the hole to release the tube completely.
5. Run your finger around the inside of the tyre to find anything sharp sticking through the tread; remove it if you find it.
6. Place the valve of the replacement tube back through the hole and replace the inner tube as far as you can.
7. Fit the lock ring loosely and pump three or four strokes of air into the tube.
8. Push more of the now partly inflated tube into the tyre and begin easing the tyre back inside the rim with your fingers, starting at the valve; remove the lock ring on the valve and push the valve deep into the tyre to make sure the tyre sits properly into the rim. Work your way round the rim until only the last few centimetres of tyre remain off the rim.
9. Hold the wheel upright on the ground and push the tyre down around the wheel to sit it firmly on to the rim. Push the rest of the tyre back with your fingers if you can, or use tyre levers if you

To mend a puncture, pump up the tyre a little and try to hear where the air is escaping. Then release the remaining air and insert a tyre lever a few inches to one side of the puncture.

Pull the tyre over the rim and clip the lever to a spoke. Then pull out a bit more tyre with the next lever, and carry on until you can extract a foot of inner tube.

The less tube you pull out, the easier the replacement will be. Sometimes the hole just can't be found, in which case you'll have to remove the whole tube. Whether you've removed just part or the whole tube, pump air back into it.

Listen for escaping air. If you can't see the hole, feel for the escaping air on the sensitive area of your top lip or on your eye.

can't. (Take care with tyre levers that you don't pinch the inner tube; the idea of partly pumping is to make pinching less likely.)

10. Replace the lock ring and pump the tyre to half pressure.
11. Settle the tyre on the rim and spin the wheel, watching the tread for any irregularities; if there are any, re-seat the tyre without deflating it if you can, otherwise let out enough air to make the job possible.
12. Put the wheel back into the frame and finish the pumping.

When you're ready to mend the puncture, you do it like this:

1. Pump up the inner tube (it will expand alarmingly) and listen for escaping air.
2. Mark the hole with a ballpoint pen and a large cross.
3. Deflate the inner tube.
4. If it's a butyl tube (artificial rubber), remove the shiny surface by rubbing vigorously with sandpaper; rub an area larger than the patch you'll use. If it's a rubber tube, go straight on to the next step.

Pay particular attention to old patches, which can sometimes come loose and let air escape gently.

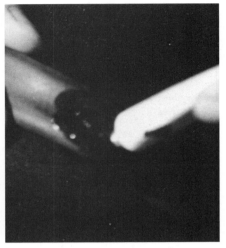

When you've found the hole, put your finger on it or better still mark it with a ballpoint. Now scour the rubber over an area half as big again as the patch you plan to use. Use the sandpaper to rub vigorously at the tube; do it too softly and the tube will be too shiny for the patch to stick.

Now spread a generous amount of puncture kit solution over the roughed-up area, spreading it into a thin, even coat with your fingertip.

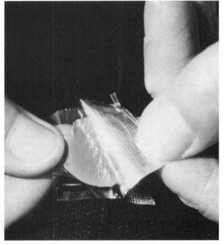

The glue must be absolutely clean and perfectly dry. It will take two minutes in dry weather but you can speed things up by blowing. Bear in mind that the solution dries inefficiently in rain.

Take the patch and peel off the metal covering that protects the dry solution. Leave the other side, if there is one.

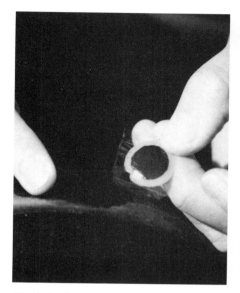

Check the dryness of the solution . . .

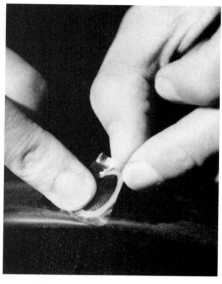

. . . and press the patch firmly, gently and evenly on to the tube, with the hole exactly in the centre.

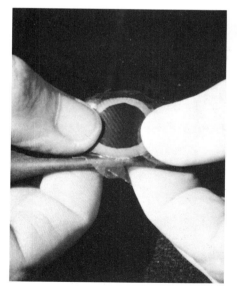

A patch will fail if you don't squeeze the edges down hard.

When you're convinced it's stuck, squeeze the patch and the inner tube into as tight a fold as you can. The backing paper should then split.

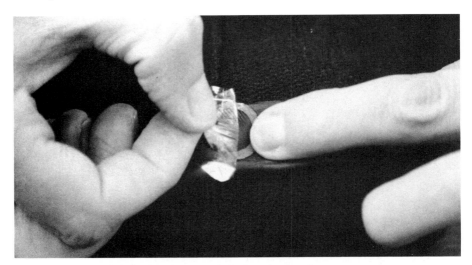

Peel off the halves of the backing paper and check again that the edges of the patch are firmly stuck down. If they're not, you can't use a dab of solution to repair the damage — you'll have to start all over again.

Scrape the tiny block of chalk in your kit on to the edge of the box.

Tip the chalk on to the remains of the dried solution to neutralize it. If you don't, there's a chance the solution will stick to the inside of the tyre itself. Now push the inner tube valve back into its hole, put the inner tube roughly back into the rim, and push as much of the tyre back into place with your fingers as you can. When no more will go in by hand, pump in a couple of strokes of air and use the tyre levers to force the rest into place, taking great care not to nip the inner tube (which is why you pumped in a few puffs of air).

5. Rub solution (glue) thinly over an area larger than the patch, with the hole in the middle, and spread the solution still more thinly with your finger.
6. Let the solution dry *completely*.
7. Peel the backing metal, but not the paper, off a patch and press the adhesive side to the dried solution; hold it firmly with your fingers for a few seconds.
8. Bend the patch until the backing paper snaps and peel it away; your puncture's then mended.

A shipped chain (one that comes off the chainring or sprocket either because it's old and stretched or because the gears are maladjusted) is no more than the messy job of tugging it from wherever it's jammed and putting it back in place.

A broken spoke can be replaced on the road by unwinding it from the nipple at one end and poking it back through the rim hole at the other, rethreading the new spoke and tightening it in place at the nipple with a spokespanner. It's a job much easier to describe than

To shorten, extend or repair a chain, you really need a specialized chain rivet extractor – nothing else will do. Fortunately, they're not expensive.

Fit the appropriate part of the chain into the slots of the tool. Now turn the handle gently until the punch exactly meets the centre of the pin that runs through the middle of a link.

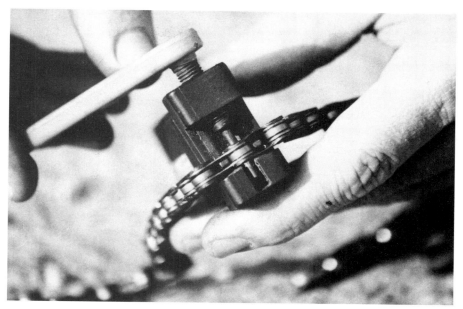

Turn carefully, testing frequently . . .

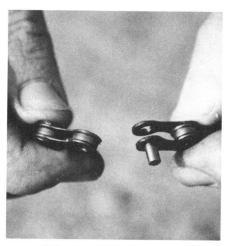

. . . until the pin is held only by its very tip. (If you press too far, the pin will drop out and only bodging will get it back in again – you have to reassemble the chain and start again.)

Now either cut out a whole section to shorten the chain, or add a male to a female link to lengthen it. If this sounds complicated, rest assured that a look at the chain and twenty seconds' thought makes it obvious.

To reassemble the chain, work from the opposite side. Push the halves together until you get a gentle fit . . .

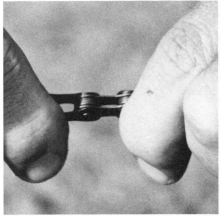

. . . put them back into the gadget and gently screw the pin back into place. Stop if you meet any resistance – it means you haven't lined up the two halves correctly and you may damage the link. Go back to the previous stage and start again.

Screw the pin back until an equal amount shows on each side.

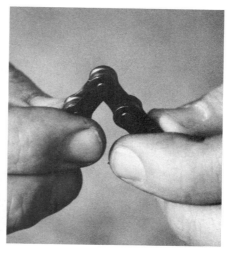

Remove the chain and flex it sideways . . .

. . . and this way . . .

. . . until you have a perfect chain with an invisible join.

*Simple spoke adjustments
are within the range of an
amateur, but you do need
a proper spoke key. Use
pliers only in an
emergency.*

complete, however; a spoke that's too long might not tighten completely or, worse, will poke through and puncture the tube. There's also a very good chance that the nipple thread has jammed, forcing you to remove the wheel and the tyre to fit another one from the inside. And then, worst of all, a spoke that breaks on the gear side of the back wheel forces you to remove the whole freewheel assembly to get at it. I've already said that this really is a job for a shop. You can lessen breakages by having your wheels rebuilt before you go off on a long holiday, or just rebuilt anyway with quality spokes if you're not sure when the job was done last. Tell your dealer if you plan to carry luggage and he'll fit stronger spokes.

Bike shops closed by the gross in the 1970s but many deserved to go. Those that have replaced them, while not as numerous, are often better quality. There are lists of recommended dealers in the CTC handbook. Phone to explain your predicament and most dealers will do their best to help a traveller in distress, even if it means your waiting a bit.

The worst disaster is to lose your bike. Few locks advertised as unbreakable live up to that description – as one maker found when a trading standards officer picked his 'top security' lock in thirty seconds and fined him £500. It's galling to discover that induction-hardened manganese steel pliers costing just £15 will cut through supposedly impossible locks costing three times as much.

It's possible to grow paranoid and assume that it's *your* bike the thieves are after. The truth is that they want any bike they can shift quickly and then sell. You have no control over the second but you have over the first. For all that it seems sensible to lock your bike up an alley-way or some other dark place, the truth is that it's not. It only takes a moment to break a lock, but it's a moment the thief prefers to spend unobserved. Even the least inquiring passer-by is likely to notice a villain working with bolt-cutters in the middle of the High Street.

> **Rule 20** *Lock your bike to something unmovable and stronger than the lock. Remove the front wheel and lock it to the frame if it's also easily moved.*

A long chain and a secure lock are essential. This is a medium-weight chain, coated in plastics to stop it scratching.

9

The Art of Cycling

The first inclination when you start cycling is to hug the very edge of the road, feeling that you haven't the nerve, the will and the brashness to stake your claim further out. But the price of staying jammed to the left is a wearying, bumpy ride, punctures from the debris, and nowhere to manoeuvre.

This brings us to

> **Rule 21** *Never ride at the edge of the road.*

You're entitled to be where you are. Hiding by the kerb encourages poor drivers to pass too close, too fast, or to overtake where it would be better not to. Ride a yard into the road. Cyclists travel on the left because *everybody* travels on the left, not because they're inferior. On the other hand, you have an obligation to let faster traffic pass with minimum inconvenience when it's safe and convenient to do so. A wave works wonders if you delay another road-user. On some lanes there's nowhere you can go to help a driver pass. It's worse uphill because you're that much slower. A wave to a fellow human being is appreciated.

So is eye contact. Turning right is difficult. It relies on someone letting you out. Your cycling proficiency teacher said to look over your shoulder, wait for a gap, extend your right arm, and move out. Well, this was fine when there were gaps to be had. Things have changed. If you see a gap, so much the better. But in continuous traffic the chances are that (*a*) you won't, and that (*b*) in town the passing traffic won't be going much faster than you. So use eye contact, the friendly approach. Look over your shoulder, catch the driver's eye, raise your hand beside your shoulder while still looking at him (like a child waiting to ask a question) and, when you've established the driver's watching you and understands what you mean, extend your arm with a wave of confirmation. Nine times out of ten, you'll be allowed out, after which you wave in thanks.

What terrifies drivers are timid cyclists who hug the kerb and switch suddenly around parked cars instead of either holding their line or moving out over a long distance at a shallow angle; and/or who jab out their right arm without looking backwards, hoping the saintly values of the Highway Code will bear them safely to the crown. My friends, it doesn't happen. If you want to be treated like a decent human being, behave like one. This remains a humane world and a smile and a wave go a long way. Even the most mean-minded driver will be tempted to let you go your way – if only because he'd rather be shot of you.

If the whole things defeats you, ride to the junction and stop. It might hurt your pride to push your bike across the road like a pedestrian, but you're a cyclist because you enjoy cycling, not because you lust for blood and danger. If you can see how the junction might be improved for cyclists, drop a line to the town hall, especially if it's a junction you use regularly. You're a ratepayer as well, remember.

Cycle Paths

Sometimes enlightened planners have built you a sensible cycle path. But not all paths are what they seem. Many are worse than the road they follow.

Just before planners numbered roads, they fretted about cyclists riding them. There were opposing causes: the first was the rising out-door movement which put more cyclists on the road, and the other was the increase in the number but not necessarily the safety of cars and lorries. The working day was reduced to less than twelve hours and most people had Sunday free. They set out walking or cycling from the grimy towns for the freshness of the country.

The answer, the planners concluded, was paths beside main routes. Today it seems extraordinary, given that traffic was so light compared with the 1990s (although these days most people have taken a driving test, whereas then they hadn't). The first path was 2½ miles beside the Western Avenue in west London in 1935. Few of the originals survive. Most got used as parking for people who lived alongside and then, to those same people's dismay, became swallowed up when their quiet 1920s road became a 1970s highway.

Don't rush to shed a tear for vanished paths. They were (and still are) frequently more dangerous to cyclists than the roads they sought to bypass. Their replacements – often half the pavement through towns – *appear* safe while increasing the danger. Most experienced cyclists prefer not to use them. Most cycling accidents – in fact most of all traffic accidents – happen at junctions. Traffic meets at different speeds and directions. The consulting engineers Allott and Lomax established in 1991 that 7 per cent of cycling accidents are at roundabouts, half of those involving cyclists hit by an entering vehicle. In fact, two-wheelers suffer 45 per cent of all accidents at roundabouts, according to a CTC research paper.

The least likely cycling accident is to be struck from behind. Nevertheless, paths are built alongside open roads, where the danger is least, only to double the danger later on. It's expensive to tunnel under every junction for cyclists and so what happens? The cyclist preserved from a danger that doesn't exist meets a worse one he wouldn't otherwise have suffered by being led back into faster traffic when the path merges with the main road before the junction. *And*, of course, he still has the junction itself to negotiate.

'All too often,' says Richard Ballantine, 'they [cycle paths] were built to get bikes out of the way of cars, not for bikes to run on.' How true. A main road has priority over side-roads. Drivers on the side-road wait for a gap in the passing traffic. Since the path is part of the main road it would be reasonable for approaching traffic to give way to that as well. In Holland that would be the case. But in Britain it's not. Therefore, as well as having to give way every hundred yards or so, the cyclist on the supposedly safer path is forced to negotiate a potentially dangerous position with cars from the left.

As if that weren't enough, lack of priority means traffic from behind on the main road no longer waits for the cyclist to cross the junction before turning left into the side road. Every side turning, therefore, has to be treated not as the secondary junction it would have been on the main road, with traffic showing precedence, but as a four-way junction. A cyclist with faster traffic on his right ready to cut across him is in the same position as one wanting to turn right across a busy road – except that on a cycle path he has to do it every hundred yards *and* with drivers who aren't expecting him to be there. Not a happy position.

There are votes these days in money for better cycling, but not many and not much. Most paths have a worse surface than the highway beside them, and even segregated cycling lanes on some town roads are too narrow for one cyclist to overtake another. So, if you want to, you're pushed out into the path of drivers who aren't expecting you. As the CTC campaigner John Franklin urges: 'Always be discriminating and cautious.'

> **Rule 22** *Take advantage of facilities where they help you, but ignore those that don't.*

Cycle paths are rarely compulsory. It takes special legislation to remove cyclists from the highway and you have the choice of whichever route or surface you prefer. In some towns, cycle paths are no more than parking strips and routes for milk floats and mail vans. In others, they're far better – wider and sometimes shared with pedestrians. The number and seriousness of accidents between cyclists and pedestrians on these paths has never been proved to be significant, although there's no reason to prove the doubters right by hurtling along them at racing speed. I always marvel how in Belgium, where racing cyclists have the status of Premier Division footballers in England, great steaming masses of high-speed cyclists sweep past basket-laden shoppers in apparent mutual safety. Only a thin yellow line prevents a considerable drain on the Belgian national health service. Cycle paths are usually – in fact, nearly always – compulsory abroad.

Fortunately, most roads are safe and drivers are honourable, good or bad just as cyclists and pedestrians are good and bad. And some, of course, would rather be out there with you on the bike.

Campaign Groups

The CTC checks councils' policies through local advisers. It has to be consulted whenever the Highway Code is changed; and it's still the only national cycling body officially notified of changes in access. The role of the CTC in keeping alight the beacon of cycling since the late 19th century has been out of all proportion to its membership. An MP once felt cyclists in his constituency to be of such little importance that he dismissed them as 'excrescences' during a debate in the Commons. Times have changed – fortunately.

You can help improve cycling in your own area by becoming one of the CTC's local advisers or joining one of the other campaign groups. Many towns have their own organizations, with colourful names such as Spokes or Saddlebags. The CTC itself has its Cyclists' Rights Network, checking, advising and often challenging road schemes and 'improvements'. The work they do is invaluable in reminding councillors and planners that many of their road problems would diminish if they promoted cycling rather than driving. Peterborough and

Stevenage have a healthier population and clearer roads because good conditions for cycling mean far more people cycle to work than the national average.

You can contact your local campaign organization through CTC headquarters or through the Cycle Campaign Network at Tress House, Stamford Street, London SE1 (tel.: 0171-928 7220). Friends of the Earth is also a strong supporter for better conditions for biking.

Accidents and Court Cases

If you do have an accident, the CTC suggest you list nine points.

1. The name and address of the driver or whoever else was involved.
2. The number and description of the other vehicle and the details of the driver's insurance certificate, if it's available.
3. The names and addresses of witnesses.
4. The time and place, including the name of the road.
5. Any personal injury, or damage to either vehicle.
6. Whether any signals were given, and whether the other vehicle showed its correct lights.
7. Draw a rough sketch of where the vehicles were before and after the accident.
8. Rough measurements of the width of the road, and whether there were any special points such as a zebra crossing, traffic lights, corner, narrow bridge and so on.
9. Take a photograph if possible of any pothole or bad road surface which caused a crash.

It's usually as quick and easy to sue through the small claims court (actually just a procedure of the county court) if you're claiming less than £500. That's often the CTC solicitor's advice. Court officials will help fill in the form but they can't give legal advice, so their manner can sometimes appear cold. It's not their fault. The CTC solicitor will help members do the job. The court charges about £30, repaid with any damages. If, on the other hand, the case fails and there are no damages, then there'll be no return fee either. In that case, the CTC will reimburse it to members.

The oddest case the CTC ever fought was for women in breeches. They were insulted as sluts or had sticks pushed through their wheels. The spirited Mrs E. Kennard, who wrote a book in 1896 called *A Guide*

Book for Lady Cyclists, was once heckled by factory girls while wearing knickerbockers and sent for a constable to deal with them. Three years later, Viscountess Harberton, president of the Rational Dress Society, was turfed out of the coffee bar of the Hautboy Hotel in Ripley, Surrey, and sent (great insult) to the public bar instead because of her scandalous dress (vast baggy trousers). She engaged the CTC to fight the case on her behalf, lost at the second hearing but won a great deal of publicity for her cause.

There is nothing more for Lady Harberton to worry about. Nor are there modern Henry Cracknells. He was fined £5 for flinging a bolas of strings and weights from the St Albans mail coach and toppling the entire Trafalgar Bicycle Club from their penny-farthings. The reason: cyclists' mobility was a threat to the carriage trade.

But by far the biggest victory was the right to cycle in the first place. There was a time when the police made the most of each county's indecision about whether cycling was even legal. The Highways and Locomotives (Amendment) Act allowed counties to do whatever they liked about cycling, and some took against it with enthusiasm. Constables jumped out on cyclists just as, forty years later, they dropped out of trees to halt motorists driving faster than 12mph. Not until the CTC lobbied cycling MPs did Westminster declare all forms of bicycle and tricycle 'to be carriages within the meaning of the Highway Acts'.

The CTC boasted titled gents and their ladies as members and reminded its less aristocratic brethren of this so they could boast to their unconverted friends. It also proved useful in changing the law, both to stop bolas-flinging mailmen and to allow Mayfair gentry to exercise in Hyde Park in 1896. But the bicycle was born too late for its own good. The petrol engine followed hard behind and the nobs abandoned the thrilling bicycle for the still more spectacular motor car.

The CTC, its members deserting and no more able to make its mind up about cars than anyone else, resolved to follow the trend. There were in its more vocal membership those who fancied a drive and wanted the CTC to represent all road users and not simply the minority, as they rightly saw it, who'd stay loyal to the bike. *Cycling* changed briefly to *Cycling and Moting* (the name of the fascinating new hobby was as uncertain as its future, but publishers could still spot a market; decades later, readers were equally horrified when they flirted equally disastrously with mopeds).

Anyway, in 1906 the CTC went to the High Court to change its constitution to look after motoring affairs as well. A poll had shown 10,495

THE ART OF CYCLING

for and only 2,231 against. If it hadn't been for the judge guessing the future and ruling that the CTC could never adequately speak for cyclists and motorists at the same time, things would have been very different. The CTC would have gone the way of other travel organizations and become no more than a part-time job for someone in the motoring club.

There was, though, a sequel. As Alan Harlow recalls: 'Mr E.R. Shipton, who had my job from 1883 to 1907, left after this court case and joined with others in setting up the AA, a link with the CTC that the AA happily acknowledge – to the disgust of our more rabidly anti-motoring members.'

10

Abroad Starts at Calais

At twelve I had a friend who had a friend Who Had Cycled Abroad. That was hero status. He lived in a bungalow, which made him much grander than us in the neighbouring council houses. My parents said he had Cycled Abroad because his family was posh, and I hadn't because we weren't posh and anyway, you stupid kid, where d'you think we're going to get the money from for something like that? Since then I've realized that cycling abroad is no more than cycling here plus a little thought and a change of language – as far as the problems are concerned, anyway. That's a tiny price for the excitement. And the financial price, once you've got Abroad, is rarely more and often less than in Britain. Trains run under the Channel more and more frequently. You can take a bike on both Eurostar (the through service from London to Paris or Brussels) and on the Shuttle (from Folkestone to Calais), thanks to negotiations by the CTC and the European Cyclists' Federation. You book-a-hook in advance on Eurostar – and cross-Channel trains carry rather more bikes than their domestic neighbours – or turn up for the Shuttle and put your bike in a cage trailer which will be towed behind the mini-bus that takes you on and off the train. You cross the Channel sitting in the bus.

By Train and Boat

Ferries remain easiest. You just buy a ticket and go. The bike is often free. Go through passport control as late as possible, because hanging about in the bluster and fumes of the port is horrible. Go to the head of the queue and ride on to the ship. The harbour and ferry staff would rather have you aboard first. There's never anywhere special to stow your bike, so place the wheels inside the shallow steel rim that runs just inside the wall of the ship itself and fasten your bike with an elastic strap to a pipe or stanchion. Remember to take a strap because

Bike bags have come a long way in recent years. They're bigger, brighter and lighter. These are light Carradice bags, on a bike kitted up for a camping journey round the world. Remember to keep clothes separate from tools, food and tent – and keep your everyday gear on the front of the bike, where it can be removed easily.

otherwise there'll only be a greasy rope hanging from a hook. Insist on leaving your bike protected from sea spray. You can't return to the car deck once the ship's at sea, so take everything with you.

The shortest crossing is Dover–Calais, followed by the other French ports and then by Ostend. Ask about day-return tickets. They're often cheaper than a single fare and how the ferry company discovers you've left the ship, I don't know. Avoid tickets with the word 'cruise' – they're for folk who want to booze both ways and have no intention of leaving the ship at turnaround.

Buy a ticket in advance if you want a cabin (essential on long night crossings). Otherwise, buy it at the port or at a garage on the approach to Dover. The price is the same, the chances of losing it much reduced. Bookings are essential for hovercraft, which are also prone to disruption in bad weather. Hovercraft also don't use the main ship-ping port, and in France the hoverport can be some distance away.

The longest south-eastern crossings are to Belgium. Harwich to Hoek van Holland or Felixstowe to Zeebrugge is six or seven hours and worth doing at night so you can sleep your way over. Long cross-ings demand a cabin anyway. Never trust a reclining seat if you want more than three minutes' sleep; it's better to pay for the seat if you have to and sleep on the floor with a couple of blankets.

At the other end, reclaim your bike, bang the roof of any motorist unkind enough to start his engine before the bow doors open, and ride off. Go straight to the front of what remains of customs and passport controls – again, port officials prefer you out of the way – and ride into Abroad. From here on, you're on the right. It's about now you realize your lights have to be moved over before nightfall.

You don't need a visa for anywhere in the European Union if you're British, Irish or another EU nationality. You also shouldn't need a pass-port, but by 1995 the British government still hadn't reached agreement with its neighbours, so you'll still need one. One-year visi-tors' cards are also being withdrawn. Ten-year passports take several weeks to issue in high summer. You can hire firms to do the hanging about for you; it's ridiculous that such people should be able to make a living, but such is the system.

Getting to the port by train means following the general rules for train travel. There are boat trains from London (Liverpool Street) to Harwich, and trains from London to Dover. Ramsgate, Sheerness and Felixstowe are fiddly to reach. Hull is some distance from the station. Check you can take a bike on the train you want. Check, too, whether you can register it through from London to Holland or France and fur-ther. British Rail's international inquiries are at Victoria Station, London SW1V 1JY (tel.: 0171-834 2345, but often with a delay, so hang on). Credit card bookings are on 0171-828 0892.

Registering means sticking on a label and paying a fee in Britain and seeing your bike again at your destination. It's reliable but I've had paintwork scratched or mudguards bent. Never register beyond Paris. Stations there are several miles apart. You can arrive at one Paris station and catch the Métro to the other, but your bike goes on a lorry and turns up in Nice or Toulouse several days after you. The trick, therefore, is to send the bike several days ahead of you (remembering that on the return journey you'll either have to do the same or be without in Britain), or register to Paris, collect it there, cycle to the other station and re-register it or simply buy a ticket to your French destination.

Why register at all? Well, on boat trains it might be essential (ask British Rail). And while you can usually avoid boat trains (the one to Dover has ended, anyway), the bike system in France is as complicated as here. Registering makes sure it gets there. Ask French Railways (SNCF) for information. They're at 179 Piccadilly, London W1V 0BA (tel.: 0171 493 9731); ask for the folder *Guide du Train et du Vélo*, and for information on registering.

If you keep your bike, ask whether a simple ticket or registration is necessary. If a ticket, load the bike aboard as in Britain. If registration, go to the door marked *bagages* or *bagages (consigné)*, pay a standard fee *and keep the ticket*. Collect the bike at the other end from the *bagages* or *bagages (arrivée)*. Should you arrive after the bike, you'll be charged left-luggage rates. You can get round that by labelling your bike *à l'avance*.

If you keep your bike all the way, remember that there are more trains from the town station in Calais than from the Maritime – and also that the French system demands you stamp your ticket at the platform before boarding the train. Dreadful things happen if you don't.

Belgian and Dutch trains are simple. Hoek van Holland and Ostend stations are alongside the ships; Zeebrugge has a station in the town but the main line at Brugge (Bruges) is half an hour away. In Holland you buy both your own and the bike's ticket at the ticket office. In Belgium, you buy your ticket there and go to the luggage office for the bike. The bike ticket comes in three parts: for you, the guard, and for the bike. Belgian prices are reasonable but Dutch railways charge by the kilometre, which gets pricey.

Belgian railways are at 10 Greycote Place, London SW1P 1SB (tel.: 0171-222 8866) and Dutch railways are at 25–28 Buckingham Gate, London SW1E 6LD, along with the tourist office. Irritatingly, you can't ring the Dutch tourist office except for a recorded announcement. You can, though, book a hotel anywhere in Holland by ringing 00-31-70-3175454; say, when, where and what price hotel and they'll do the rest. That's helpful because Dutch hotels are infrequent and full, and it saves waiting until you get to a Dutch tourist office (VVV) and finding the hotels are full and you've got to pay the VVV a commission. I expect the international service sticks the commission on when you pay at the hotel, but at least you *feel* you're getting something for nothing.

There's also a hotel service for Dover, tel.: 01304-212512. Dover Priory station is ten minutes from Eastern docks (turn right downhill and follow the signs). You could once travel from London to a platform alongside your ship. And there, in the shadow of toffs and their ladies boarding paddle-steamers and putteed soldiers doing much the same (although without the parasols) in 1914, you boarded the ferry.

By Air

Going by air depends on the airline. There is no uniformity and it's important to ask whether you need a box, or if the bike will be weighed, or measured, or just counted as an item of luggage. Even companies on the same route have different policies.

At its easiest, you have only to turn up and present the bike at the check-in desk. Airline clerks sometimes think they're still registering Neville Chamberlain to fly to Herr Hitler and forget that baggage holds are pressurized these days and have bigger doors than in the days of the DC3. Loading staff prefer to wheel the bike to the plane and not balance it on a pile of suitcases. Check-in clerks, on the other hand, feel you should strap the wheels to the frame, turn the handle-bars through 90 degrees, deflate the tyres and reverse the pedals.

The loading argument will usually keep your wheels in place. Most clerks can also be persuaded that modern pedals don't reverse. But it's rare to win the deflated tyres debate, which is a pain when you have to pump them up again at the other end. Compromise by letting out some of the air, but not all, so that bike won't bump on its rims and pinch the inner tubes as it's pushed or dropped on the conveyor belt. You'll have to pay for a box if the airline insists on it. Dealers get their new bikes from the factory in similar boxes and your shop might get you a free one. Otherwise take a roll of sticky tape with you and fasten some rolled-up newspaper around the paintwork.

A bike with luggage will usually fit the 44-pound (20kg) weight limit, unless you're camping. Bikes are too difficult to weigh, and check-in clerks have no idea how heavy a bicycle is. They just want to get you out of the way, so I've never known anyone pay excess baggage. A bike does have to be handled specially, so help the airline by turning up in extra time. Tell the reservations staff in advance if there is a party of you. Ask for confirmation in writing, since airline head offices are rarely at the airport and the helpful man who promised you everything on the phone won't be around when you meet a check-in clerk with a headache, domestic problems and a foul temper. And remember that tandems and tricycles defeat normal baggage procedure, and that package-holiday operators might need tactful handling. Tell them in advance that you're bringing a bike to avoid disappointment at the airport.

All British airports are simple to enter except Heathrow. If you're not careful, you'll end up in the motorway tunnel. There's a bike tunnel at the end of the cycle path which runs to the terminals from the Newport Road roundabout on the A4. Terminals 1, 2 and 3 are inside the airport; 4 is close to the A30, outside the runways, on the southeastern side. There are trains from London Victoria to Gatwick and from Liverpool Street to Stansted, but check with British Rail (tel.: 0171-730 3400) about taking a bike. There are two Victoria–Gatwick rail services, at different prices.

Money

Use a credit card or Eurocheques abroad. They're cheaper and easier than travellers' cheques. With good luck, a credit card payment in, say, Belgium, will take a month to reach your account in Britain and another month to appear on your statement. Electronic tills speed it up a bit, but there's still a delay and the exchange rate is often better than for tourists. Access (Eurocard/Mastercharge) and Visa are widely accepted abroad, although less in Holland than other countries. Cards are known by different names in different countries – Carte Bleu is the most common in France, for example – but all belong to central clearing organizations. Showing the small emblems on the back of your credit card will usually do the trick.

Domestic cheques aren't valid abroad and you'll need Eurocheques. The bank charges to issue them and again to cash them, so use them sparingly. Their benefit is that they can be written in any European country where the banks belong to the Eurocheque network, which is almost everywhere in the west. Your bank and credit cards will let you draw money from hole-in-the-wall machines in many countries; your bank will give you details. You use the same pin number.

If you do run out of money, phone your bank at home and explain the problem. Hope that the manager values your business. Money can be transferred within 15 minutes under the fastest system but always within a few hours using what the banks call their 'correspondent banks' network.

Outside Europe, use travellers' cheques. Have them either in the denomination of the country you're visiting or, if that's too complicated or numerous, in American dollars. They're more accept-able than sterling or Irish pounds. Take a small amount of foreign cash with you for tips and other minor items. Exchange rates on ships, at airports and at banks rarely differ by worthwhile amounts. Hotels and shops are often punitive, however.

In potentially dangerous areas, make arrangements with your bank to have money credited to you at intervals. It's better than carrying cash or even travellers' cheques in quantity. Travellers' cheques can't be cashed except by you, and the bank will reimburse you if they're stolen. But none of that will stop a thief who either doesn't understand the system or who knows a black-market way of doing a deal with them.

Health

Your health in EU countries is covered by an EU agreement. That doesn't mean it's free, only that you'll get the same treatment as a national. Ask the Department of Social Security or a post office for form E111, which proves your entitlement to national health treat-ment. You will almost certainly be asked to pay something for medical treatment and, for that reason, it's wise to have private medical insur-ance as well. In France, be sure to insist you're taken to a state rather than a private hospital. For anywhere outside the European Union, medical insurance, including the price of repatriation, is vital. Insure for a million pounds or more in the United States and for third-party cover of at least £2m.

CTC Tours

Remember that if you're uncertain about cycling abroad alone, there are trips organized by the CTC. They're as simple as a few days around the Dutch bulb fields and as adventurous as several weeks through the mountains of Nepal. Lists are always available from CTC headquar-ters, and they're also published annually in *CT&C*. Prices are higher than package tours, because they're individually organized, but they're no more and probably less than what you'd pay for yourself. Tour leaders are highly experienced, and party sizes are small. Many trips fill up months in advance.

11

Taking the Children, too

You don't have to stop cycling just because you've got children. Babies might be a problem, but biking can start again from the moment yours can sit upright – or even before if you buy a sidecar. I've never understood why anyone buys a sidecar, admittedly, because they're difficult enough with a motorbike. But people do, and they (or rather one particular woman from south Yorkshire did) ride unbelievably fast with them. I came across this strange silhouette late one Sunday, a quarter of a mile ahead of me; from a distance, she looked like an old-fashioned AA patrol man having a fit. She was rumbling the sidecar along so enthusiastically that it took me three miles to catch her.

Child Seats and Helmets

The benefits of taking a child with you are obvious. The child gets fresh air, new horizons and company. You get to keep on cycling. But life's never perpetual glee, so there are drawbacks. It's hard work. If you don't already have tiny gears – even down to 25 inches, which under other circumstances would be daft or dangerous – you soon will. Every hill now has to be taken in the saddle rather than by dancing on the pedals. You'll also think more about your brakes going down the other side. It's bad enough having a tight squeeze with just you on the bike; it gets worse with full touring baggage; it becomes irresponsible and potentially lethal with a passenger.

You'll need heavier spokes in the back wheel, too, and probably a heavier – say a World Touring class – of tyre. A mountain bike or a traditional tourer is better than a skittish racing bike. Imagine what happens when you place all that weight so high up and so far behind the rear hub. The bike is over-heavy at the back, which demands care until you get up enough speed for full stability.

Little padded seats on the top tube are out of the question. You need

142

something substantial, something protective, something enclosed. It has to be behind the saddle. Writing in *CT&C*, Sally Barrett, who has two children, said:

'We would recommend the high-back child seats, as they support the child asleep, and a child of three can unbalance a bike if he falls to one side. Having said that, we have always managed with low-back, old-fashioned, black steel seats, since our eldest weighed 40lb when we started and I still haven't heard of a modern seat taking more than 40lb.

'Of course, we strap them in and they now wear crash helmets. It only needs a slight blow to the skull to kill or seriously maim – a couple of times my bike has overbalanced while stationary and if the child's head had met a kerb stone there would have been a serious accident. We put our children into canoe helmets as they are fully adaptable and we could not have afforded the 5–7 bike helmets needed to fit their developing head sizes.'

Child seats carry youngsters from about nine months to about four, or, at least, to 40lb, which is the limit most makers specify. Some fit the handlebars, giving you a view of your child, but more serious versions rest across the back wheel. It might be helpful to see your passenger, it's certainly agreeable to talk to him as you go. But it's bad enough when he lolls sideways in a back seat; when he does it on the handlebars, your steering goes to pot. More than that, your passenger is putting out no effort so he'll get cold. Sitting at the front, cutting into the wind, isn't comfortable.

> **Rule 23** *Look after the passenger with more wind and cold-proofing equipment than you'd imagine.*

The best seats have high backs and side wings to keep off the worst. You provide a moderate front windbreak yourself. But just sitting still (you hope) is chilly, even on a mild day, and it gets chillier the faster you ride. The perfect cover-all – and you might have to make your own if you can't find one – has an elasticated hood that leaves only the eyes, mouth and nose free and a body envelope which generously hides everything, including the feet. And personally, though I prefer to ride without one myself, I wouldn't carry a child unless he was wearing a helmet.

It's important to use the right one. Children's heads are oversized for their bodies. They're a great weight for the child to support, so you'll be doing him no favours by buying a heavy helmet. A no-shell design that covers all the forehead and the ears is ideal. It doesn't matter that so large a helmet has poor ventilation – in fact, for someone just sitting there that's a bonus. But it is essential that it's as light as possible. The same standard certificates apply to children's helmets as to those for adults.

And please, do be sure that the seat you buy has leg guards so generous that, in even the wildest circumstances you can imagine, feet can't end up in spokes. On a mountain bike with cantilever brakes that might prove a problem causing you to shop around (try the ads in *CT&C*), but it's simpler with standard brakes. And never, ever, buy a seat which hasn't got at least crotch, waist and shoulder straps. Few people want to carry *anything* heavy, let alone a passenger, so the choice in the shops is small. You'll regret not taking the maximum time choosing the right seat.

There are other ways of carrying children – sidecars (almost unobtainable and certainly hard work), half-bikes made as self-propelling trailers (and generally called a Rann, after the firm which first made them) and straightforward trailers (imported by Burley Lite of Wadebridge, Cornwall PL27 7AX (tel.: 01208-815321), although there might also be others).

If you want the genuine family-awheel machine, contact the celebrated Pashley factory, maker of Post Office delivery bikes, shop-boy small-wheelers and the rest. No one shows more enthusiasm for bikes to carry two and, for all I know, even more children. I once visited the cycling editor Jim McGurn at his home in York and was carried back to the station on a tandem trike which customarily had a trailer fitted for his children. It was an exhilarating experience.

Children's Bikes

By the time a child can pedal for himself, he can ride a long way. He can, but he shouldn't be allowed to. I remember organizing a race in Hertfordshire once at which a spectator had ridden ten miles with his seven-year-old son. To be fair, the boy didn't look particularly tired, but he still had to ride home again, of course. That seems unreasonable for a growing body. Children recover much more slowly than adults and exhaustion is more serious. Children who don't complain at the first sign of effort will go on to ride until they drop, often without grumbling, frequently just to please their unwise parents. Please don't allow them to, for their own health, for your state of mind, and for any hope that they'll grow up as fellow-cyclists.

You can take a child cycling with stabilizers but it would be painfully slow for both of you. Stabilizers are fine for a trip to the shops or back, but no further. 'Toy' bikes are fine for getting started but they don't last. No reason why they should – children thrash bikes in a way adults can hardly imagine and a toy bike that survives that era of childhood is rarely in any condition to be passed on.

It's better to encourage proper cycling at home without stabilizers. Set the saddle so low that both the child's feet can reach the ground without effort. Then let him scoot the bike about until, by himself, he gets the hang of balance. You might need or wish to give advice or even a guiding hand now and again, but it really is better just to let him get on with it. If he just doesn't, it might simply be that he's too young or too tiny to tackle cycling for a few months.

Distances will still be tiny, of course. Think about getting a tandem for 'real' cycling. They are expensive but there are plenty of second-hand ones around – check the small ads in *CT&C* – and they keep a good resale value, assuming you don't fall in love with the thing for all the opportunity it gives you and the other parent to use it as well.

A handful of dealers sell dinky specialist kits which fit another set of pedals and a chainring just under the back saddle. Turning the pedals turns a chain which in turn drives the chainring. The child on the back can therefore contribute at least something. That's mentally and physically strengthening. The London CTC stalwarts Bob and Wendy Kynaston reversed the dropped handlebars at the back of their tandem and added a long flat U-shaped extension, well padded, so their son could hold on to something without straining forward for the normal handlebars. Ingenuity is always called for because bikes are made for adults and children aren't the right shape – or is it the bike? The so called kiddycranks kit can be moved further down the seat tube and the chain shortened as legs lengthen. But before you reach the maximum depth, the child will be off and riding a bike of his own anyway.

Children's bikes have disastrous fashions. For a while they look like smaller adults' machines, and then an overweight man in a suit will look at the sales figures and decide that what he needs is A Fresh Approach. They come every decade or so and some, thankfully, survive for less time than others. There was the Chopper, which had the riding position of a Harley-Davidson motorcyle and a twist-grip gear change to complete the illusion; to complete the mental persuasion that cycling was just a kids' way into motorcycling, the Chopper had a rear roll-bar, chopper-style handlebars, a flat seat and as little in the way of conventional cycling comfort and pleasure that the designers could concoct. Earlier generations created their own illusions by pegging a cigarette card into the spokes – or, in America of the 1930s, bought the awful Schwinn Aerocycle, which even had an imitation petrol tank on the top tube.

Then came the BMX bike, which was at least useful for performing tricks – all that it was ever advertised to do. It produced a rash of magazines, mostly American, written in backwoods English. 'Radical' became the all-purpose adjective of approval, or just 'rad' if you wanted to be truly hip. 'Is this bike radical? Heck, does a bear poop in the forest?!' asked one of the magazines' excitable reviewers.

It was all good fun, and shops sold a lot of bikes, but the trade and the sport were both glad to see the back of them. Apart from anything else, few Chopper or BMX riders progressed on to 'real' bikes, and that meant they were a retail cul-de-sac; they abandoned cycling instead. The trade says it's too cautious, too sensible, to make the same mistake again. Cynics say it'll take only a dip in the mountain-bike boom and someone, somewhere – the fat man in a suit – will be tempted all over again. The Chopper, after all, all but saved Raleigh in the gloom of 1970. Kids will clamour for them and force their parents into buying an evolutionary cul-de-sac.

Children need shorter cranks for shorter legs. Unfortunately, the bottom bracket can't be correspondingly lower because then the pedals would hit the ground on corners. But if the bottom bracket stays high, the saddle will be even higher and short legs can't reach the ground. Therefore the rules about perfect saddle height can't apply. Compromise is essential. Children grow in spurts and a too-low saddle is as uncomfortable for them as for you. Check the saddle height every two weeks and be prepared to raise it a centimetre a time. The rule about never having less than two inches of seatpin left in the frame still applies.

If you have the money, you can get a tiny bike built to adult dimensions. A specialist shop, known in the business as a 'lightweight dealer' – the words are as much an indication of state of mind as of the shop's stock – will take care of things for you. The smallest feasible size is probably 18 inches for the frame, with 26-inch wheels. It's not cheap, but there's a good secondhand market. The writer Tim Hughes had one made and confessed: 'It was only the fact that it had about a dozen years of prospective usefulness for three children that made it, to us, an economic proposition.'

Never change the size of a bike artificially – by fixing blocks to the pedals, for instance, or changing to much shorter cranks. The same applies to reversing the handlebars. You just make the bike unbalanced and difficult or even dangerous to ride. It's a false economy. And never buy a cheap and nasty bike for your youngster just because you're afraid he won't take to cycling. Nothing is more guaranteed to make sure your fears come true. If *you* wouldn't ride a heavy, sluggish, poorly made bike, why should he? Why shouldn't he enjoy it as much as you? Rubbishy bikes have no resale value; at least you'll get a fair bit of your money back with a decent machine.

Rule 24 *Children need more stimulation than cycling alone.*

For them, simple pedalling is insufficient. They need stops not only to rest but to explore and, unbelievably, wear off excess energy. Expect short cycling days with plenty of halts – perhaps every ten minutes for young children. Speeds will be slow and distances short because, while children can put out brief spurts, their tolerance of prolonged exercise is low. And they don't always understand. I still smile at the memory of a little girl experiencing her first hill, turning to her father and protesting: 'Daddy, my pedals are getting stiff.'

I had my first bike when I was twelve, a bit older than most of my friends. I lived then on the edges of London and the roads were considered extremely dangerous. But that was by the standards of my parents, who remembered them as they'd been in the 1920s. Modern roads seem dangerous to you because you recall them from the 1960s – or, to be exact, when I was twelve. The point I'm making is that we accept the world as it is when we found it, which means children facing today's traffic have never known it different. I doubt there's any more cause to worry than in the 1960s. It just seems that there is. Cars stop and steer far better than they did. Driving standards are far higher. Drivers are much more aware of cyclists than they were thirty years ago. Fatal and serious accidents are fewer, especially compared with the increased traffic.

That doesn't mean casting youngsters on to mega-highways without a care. That would be foolish. But there are still side-roads on which to learn, and it's a rare town that doesn't have a quiet means of escape. By fourteen I was riding forty miles a day with anyone who could keep up (and sometimes with friends with whom *I* couldn't keep up!) and by sixteen I'd ridden a hundred miles or more and been on two-week cycling holidays alone. And things haven't changed that much.

12

Heck, It's Cold Out There

I came across a table once which scared the life out of me. I love cycling in the winter and there have been years that I've done more then than in summer. It's something to do with sneaking a pleasurable day when all logic says the weather's too bad to be cheerful, I suppose. The roads are emptier, the air has a crispness and the fields and trees a melancholy which rather appeals to me. There's also something doubly rewarding about getting home feeling damp but warm, with cheeks chilled by the air, to drink tea and eat buttered toast.

Wind speed plus riding speed	Air temperature (F)							
	50	40	30	20	10	0	-10	-20
5	48	37	27	16	6	-5	-15	-26
10	40	28	16	4	-9	-24	-33.5	-46
15	36	22	9	-5	-18	-32	-45	-58
20	32	18	4	-10	-25	-39	-53	-67
25	30	16	0	-15	-29	-44	-59	**-74**
30	28	13	-2	-18	-33	-48	-63	**-79**
35	27	11	-4	-20	-35	-51	-67	**-82**
40	26	10	-6	-21	-37	-53	-69	**-85**

LITTLE DANGER *RISING DANGER* **GREAT DANGER**
(Dr Ed Burke, Inside The Cyclist, Velo-News (USA) 1979)

Anyway, this table was in an American magazine and it was the most graphic illustration I've seen of how the air around you gets colder as you cycle into it. Of course, it was drawn up by a scientist, and scientists exist only to explain to you in complicated terms things which you knew perfectly well already. And, being an American scientist, he used temperatures far lower than you might expect to find on the

Nuneaton ring road in even the bitterest winter. You look at the figures and you imagine being found frozen solid in the doorway of Sainsbury's. And then you realize that you know perfectly well to wear more clothes when it's cold, and that if you still feel cold you have to put on more clothes. Logical, really.

But which clothes? You really do now need specialist cycling clothes unless you're riding just a couple of miles to work. Cycling tracksuit tops have longer backs and arms, and long zips to help ventilation. Cycling trousers are also longer at the back, and they don't have hip pockets simply because things would fall out while you're cycling. The trousers are either full length, with a zipped and elasticated ankle and narrow calf to avoid snagging the chain or catching the wind, or they end just under the knee. Either way, they're nearly always trimmed with the rainbow stripes of cycling world championships. I always slacken the elastic in the waist and wear braces instead. They keep the trousers up more securely – the bending action makes them slip down otherwise – and they avoid a sweaty band around your waist.

Both designs have advantages and drawbacks. The long style takes less explaining, but leg-tight black trousers do make you look like Max Wall or an operatic hangman, especially once they've started stretching at the knee. The knee-length breeches – plus-twos – are comical in quite another way but they're good on long showery days because you can change into clean, long socks without having to remove your trousers as well. Me, I go for the Max Wall look. The plus-twos needn't look quite so daft if you avoid the vivid diamond-pattern socks so many shops sell as cycling socks. They look like something that's come off a golf-course in the 1920s, with a smack of Bertie Wooster. Thick ski-socks in one colour are far better.

In fact, ski clothing is ideal for cycling because the two positions are nearly the same. Ski hats and gloves are perfect. Only the salopettes and padded trousers are unsuitable. Cyclists who are alike in all other ways vary in their wish for gloves and hats. I've ridden, in two pairs of gloves and a balaclava, alongside blokes with bare heads and hands. I even have two bands of knitted wool, three inches deep, to cover any gap between my sleeves and my wrists.

> **Rule 25** *If you're going to experiment either way, do it with gloves.*

You can always take them off later. Not taking them at all, and not taking a hat, can give you a nasty frost nip. So, for chaps, can riding into a sub-zero headwind for several hours. The discomfort comes when you, or at least one part of you, begins to thaw. That's when the truth of the American wind-chill table comes to mind.

> **Rule 26** *Wear long johns under your tracksuit bottoms in winter, and sew up the hole.*

A lot of experienced riders also wear racing shorts between their tracksuit and their long johns. In theory, the fewer layers between your skin and the saddle, the less chance you'll get saddle-sore. The rule holds true, but forget it when it comes to really cold weather. Long johns are necessary for men and women.

There is no reason to feel even slightly chilly in winter. Wear several thin layers rather than one thick one. Choose wool rather than man-made fabrics, unless you want to go the whole way and buy a specialist jacket which feels strangely as though it's made from the chunks of white polystyrene used to pack televisions and record players. You'll shiver a little in the first mile, or after you've been in a steam-fuggled café (cafés are always brilliant in midwinter, especially for a late breakfast with a dozen other cyclists). But after that you're warm. I did for a while carry a flimsy nylon anorak with me just in case. Some people still do. I found, though, that once I'd put it on, I could never take it off because I'd sweated so much in it.

If your feet get cold, the answer is to buy overshoes. They slip over your ordinary shoes – and they fit specialist cycling shoes best – and divert the air. A few old-timers still make their own but attach them to the toe-clips permanently. There was a fad once for wearing an extra pair of socks *over* shoes, but I think it died out due to the aggravation of cyclists' mothers. The only other trick worth a try is to put your stockinged feet into plastic bags before putting your shoes on, but frankly it looks pretty daft and your feet sweat furiously.

Cold feet and hands only last a few miles, anyway. Once they're warm, they stay warm for the rest of the day. I think it's got something to do with the brain deciding the body's cold and drawing all the surplus blood in from the extremities. Once it realizes the middle of you is pretty warm already, thanks, it lets the blood back out again. You can speed that up by walking up the first hill, which flexes your feet, operates your lower leg muscles, gives you a breather, and sends the warm blood channelling in.

I'd better mention cycling shoes here. They're worth having if you plan to ride an hour or more. They come in two patterns: racing or so-called triathlon shoes, with thick soles and light uppers with Velcro

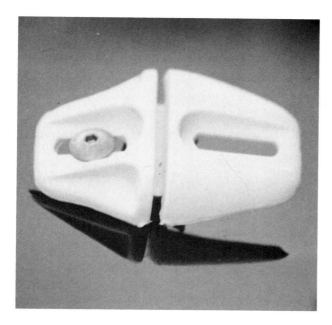

Standard cycling shoes have adjustable plates like this to grip the pedal. The bolt on the left screws into a thread set into the shoes. Some shoes have two threads, so a further slot is provided on the right.

Old-fashioned shoes still have nail-on plates. Old shoes, particularly if they have no perforations and substantial soles, are ideal for the rain and mud of winter – but use a larger size to take thicker socks, and wear two pairs of socks if it's freezing.

151

seals, or touring shoes not unlike trainers. The first are perfect for the job but so specialized that they're difficult even to walk in; the second, with their softer rubber soles and heavier uppers, are a compromise, but at least you can get off and look round a castle or an old church without walking like a duck.

Many shoes are made to lock to the pedals, either with grooved plates that clip over the back frame of the pedal, or with locking devices that match pedals made by the same company. The first need toe-clips and the second demand reliable deftness. The trend is against toe-clips and towards locking pedals and in racing circles it's already complete. The advantage to touring cyclists is that the clamping gadget can be recessed into the sole of a touring shoe, so that it neither forces your toes higher than your heels, as on racing shoes, nor makes a spectacularly loud clacking noise as you walk through a museum or art gallery. There are several sorts of locks but the most popular is made by the Japanese company Shimano. You push a small spur set in the sole against a corresponding groove in the pedal, and there it'll

Dinky pedals like this Shimano are slowly gaining popularity. Plates set into the sole of cycling shoes clip into the mechanism and stay secure until a twist of the foot releases them. They need practice.

*Shimano clipless pedals and their commercial rivals can't be
ridden on either side – the bottom is almost smooth.*

stay locked until you twist your foot at 45 degrees to release it. The
advantages – and for fastened toe-clips and straps as well – are that
you have complete control over your pedals, which you can pull up as
well as push down to help on hills. The thicker soles also keep your
feet warmer in winter. The ventilation, perforations and netting in
racing shoes don't, however, so the message is obvious.

Coping with Headlights

The winter brings darkness early and that means traffic coming the
other way with headlights. The trend for brighter and, above all,
square rather than round headlamps means more light spills from
them than before. Drivers concentrating on what's happening on their
side of the road can't or won't look over to yours for the pinprick of
light from your lamp. Some just don't care anyway.

153

> **Rule 27** *If you're dazzled on a main road, keep looking down at the edge of the road beside you.*

If you lose it, gamble on going to the right rather than coming to a stop. Stopping takes a distance to do, in which time you might hit something or run off the road or just lose your balance. There's no problem about drifting out to the right if you're dazzled because anything coming from behind will have headlights that will cancel the dazzle and light up the road for you again. But wander to the left and you hit the kerb or the verge. Provided you resist the temptation to look up, there's usually no problem.

> **Rule 28** *Close your eyes when the car's alongside you and the momentary blackness will open your irises again for the darkness ahead.*

If you don't, your eyes will be pinpricks fighting off the headlights and they'll expand too slowly to cope with the change.

Drivers approaching you on smaller roads are more likely to dip their lights because you're in their field of view. Some are just arrogant or it doesn't occur to them that you might find it uncomfortable or even dangerous being pinned there like a motorway rabbit, in which case you can ride towards the headlights with a theatrical waving of the arms and shielding of the eyes. Most drivers eventually get the message, if only because it's a surprise to see a gesticulating idiot out on a bike so late at night.

If you just can't see anything, ride straight for the headlights but very slowly, still gesticulating. If nothing else, you know that the headlights are on the road. And being right in front of the driver forces him to pay attention to you. It's safe enough because headlights reach several hundred metres and, if there's the slightest chance of being mown down, you can escape to either side long before it happens. These are all extreme cases, though, and in general night riding is tiring but tolerable.

Ice

What is genuinely scary is ice. Ice in the morning will often melt within a couple of hours. But ice in later afternoon is there to stay. The standard advice is to relax, ride in a straight line, and not to brake. But about the only places in Britain you can do that are the Fens and the Somerset Levels. Everywhere else the roads twist and go downhill and you can't go downhill without braking. There is no answer to ice except not to be out on it. It forms more on side-roads and lanes because they're not salted. It forms on bridges because there's no warmth beneath them. And it forms in hollows (hence the braking) rather than hill-tops, and it can lie there invisible even by daylight.

There was once a popular cyclists' café near Hatfield, in Hertfordshire, called the Marshmoor. It stood on the old Great North Road near a gentle right-hand bend down a shallow hill. Nothing on that road suggested ice. It was daylight, it was sunny and the road looked just as it had every other day. And yet I fell off, and my mates Dave and Tony also fell off. And when we stood up and waved to other cyclists following us and distracted their attention by shouting, they too fell off. Several dozen other riders all fell off within eight minutes. I don't know what you can do about days like that – or about thick fog – except not go out in them. You can ride in snow that's just a few inches thick and you can ride in torrential rain, but fog and ice are good reasons to go by bus instead.

Night Riding

Night riding in summer is a wholly different experience, although quite often chilly as well. Night in winter is eerily quiet and the cold air denies you scents. In summer it's different. I had a habit some years ago of deliberately riding right through the night, or at least leaving home before dawn. It was sublime. The lanes are deserted after midnight and traffic returns only from about 7.30, or later at weekends. It's quite true that the best time of the day is just before most people think about going out. All the usual caution of nature goes into abeyance in early mornings; creatures unaccustomed to humans at night feel safe enough in the dark, and rabbits will congregate on the road by the dozen until you're almost on top of them. I once came across a duck leading its young in a neat line across my path and stopped to let them pass. There was neither hurry nor concern.

Riding through the night is a good way of ending or starting a cycling holiday, although you have to remember you'll be that much more tired not the next day but the day after that. The route you take doesn't have to be as complicated as it might be by day, when you're escaping the traffic, and it's just as well because map-reading by night is a pain. Avoid the main roads, certainly, but go for B-roads instead.

Night riding gives you the impression of travelling faster than you are. It's because your vision extends only to the close by, which whizzes past, and it's denied the compensation of the slower-moving horizon. That's fine because it keeps you cheerful, but it's galling to find that ten miles still takes as long to ride as ever it did.

And don't be tricked into thinking that it'll be warm all night. Summer nights are comfortable enough for shorts if it's been warm by day and the sky is cloudy enough to keep the warmth in. But temperatures fall fast if the sky's clear and the old saying about the hour before dawn being both the darkest and coldest is true. I say this from experience. I rode once from north London to Eastbourne at night just for the heck of it, and by East Grinstead in mid-Sussex I was shivering as I rode. A few miles later, in the clammy Ashdown Forest, I was stopped by a swinging red light at a police road block. They were looking for an escaped inmate from a borstal and, while they were convinced I wasn't their convict, they were equally sure I was giving them cheek by saying I'd ridden fifty miles to that point from north London. Nobody cycled fifty miles at night in shorts and a cotton shirt, they thought.

I don't know how I persuaded them but they must have taken pity on me because they gave me coffee from their flasks, which kept me warm for another ten miles until I was so utterly cold that I pulled on my cape and crouched in a telephone kiosk with a roadmender's hurricane lamp for warmth. It was a miserable half-hour until dawn. My compensation was a day on the beach and riding along Beachy Head, and an attic room at Alfriston youth hostel in which I found dozens of dead but preserved butterflies still clinging to the windows. Gory but beautiful.

13

The End of the Road

And that's about it, really. Happy cycling.

I'm writing this as an addict. I stole my sister's push-scooter when I was eight and graduated to a bike four years later. Within a couple of years I'd abandoned family holidays and gone off by myself each summer, bank holidays and weekends as well. I learned a lot, not just about the world but about me. I came to realize pretty quickly that I was no natural athlete, that I could get horribly tired on a bike, and that the thing about cycling was that you always had to get home afterwards. It didn't matter how long you sat on a roadside seat feeling cream-crackered and self-pitying, the same number of miles still separated you from home. I'm hoping these self-imposed lessons in self-dependence might save you learning them all over again.

There have been millions of cyclists over the years. I can't, as Les Warner (the secretary who saw the CTC through the lean years of the 1960s and 1970s) said 'think of a more blameless but more misunderstood hobby'. The experience of all those blameless and misunderstood millions have led to the CTC, the oldest touring organization in the world and the only one still dedicated solely to cyclists.

Or perhaps I shouldn't say 'blameless'. We've had the less than perfect in our midst since the start. The *Glasgow Argus* of 9 June 1839 contains this report of the celebrated Kirkpatrick Macmillan, who shares equal fame and notoriety for the twin (and unprovable) claims of having made the world's first back-wheel-drive bicycle . . . and having had the first cycling accident.

'On Wednesday a gentleman who stated he came from Thornhill in Dumfries, was placed at the Gorbals public bar, charged with riding along the pavement on a velocipede to the obstruction of the passage, and with having, by so doing, thrown over a child. It appeared from his statement that he had on the day previous come all the way from Old Cumnock, a distance of forty miles, bestriding the velocipede, and that he performed the journey in the space of five hours.

'On reaching the Barony of Gorbals, he had gone upon the pavement, and was surrounded by a large crowd, attracted by the novelty of the machine. The child who was thrown down had not sustained any injury, and under the circumstances the offender was fined only 5 shillings. The velocipede employed in this instance was very ingeniously constructed – it moved on wheels, turned with the hand by means of a crank; but to make it "progress" appeared to require more labour than will be compensated for by the increase of speed.

'This invention will not supersede the railway.'

I shall file that along with *The Engineer* of February 1890, which looked very quizzical about these new-fangled pump-up tyres: 'Considerable difficulty will be experienced in keeping the tyres thoroughly inflated [and] they are prone to slip on muddy roads. . . . The appearance of the tyres destroys the symmetry and graceful appearance of a cycle, and this alone is, we think, sufficient to prevent their coming into general use.'

Or then again, this from a Mrs D. Woodland of Edgware, Middlesex, to her twelve-year-old son, circa 1959: 'We've got you this bike but your father and I can't see you'll ever stick to it, so if you don't ride it we'll take it back and sell it.' The world, you see, has never considered cyclists properly.

Index

Numbers in italics denote illustrations